Betty Crocker's
American Country
Cooking

Random House / New York

American Country Cooking is a collection of recipes we as Americans share as our culinary heritage. These recipes are reminders of the homespun traditions of yester-year. And just as some of us surround ourselves with country furnishings because they are comfortable, we treasure recipes from times past because they link us to our ethnic roots and remind us of the diversity of our regional backgrounds.

Because our families may be miles apart and generations removed from grandma's kitchen, we like to collect bits and pieces from the past that help us feel closer to each other. We stir a pot of peach preserves with grandma's sturdy wooden spoon or cut molasses-tinged *Joe Froggers* with cookie cutters found in a country antique shop. A bride takes home her new family's prized recipe for *Raspberry Jam Cake,* carrying with her the key to a priceless Christmas tradition. Each of us remembers a special dish our mother used to cook, something her own mother and grand-mother prepared for her, and we continue that tradition by preparing that same dish for our loved ones.

But, we ask, where did these recipes come from and how did they get their unusual names? Listeners from fifty years ago had the same questions when they tuned their radios to *Betty Crocker's The Gold Medal Hour.* This series of programs on American cooking was immensely popular. People learned the history behind why the Cajuns of Louisiana find crawfish as ordinary as the baked beans Bostoners eat on Saturday nights. They found out how a yellowed and crumbling news clipping with the recipe for *Soldier's Fudge* got its name. Even then, families felt they were losing touch with the stories that surrounded old-time recipes and were entranced by the answers to their questions.

Our curiosity about down-home recipes from the past continues today with the same delight and fascination shown by those listeners years ago. They are what you requested when asked by the Betty Crocker Kitchens what to include in this cookbook. They are the recipes and stories that are America's best.

Betty Crocker's American Country Cooking is a way to turn back the clock to all the pleasures that awaited us in grandma's kitchen. Just turning the pages of *Betty Crocker's American Country Cooking* will be like going home to the wonderful aromas of our past.

The Betty Crocker Editors

Editors, Kay Emel-Powell, Lois L. Tlusty; Recipe Development Editor, Mary Hallin Johnson; Recipe Editor, Kristine Schwappach; Food Styling Coordinator, Cindy Lund; Food Stylists, Katie W. McElroy, JoAnn Cherry, Lynn Lohmann; Art Directors, Gerald Goodge, John Currie; Project Managers, Sue Kersten, Lynette Reber; Prop Styling, Larue Despard; Photographer, Nanci E. Doonan

Copyright © 1987 by General Mills, Inc., Minneapolis, Minnesota. All rights reserved under International and Pan-American Copyright Conventions. Published in the United States by Random House, Inc., New York, and simultaneously in Canada by Random House of Canada Limited, Toronto.

Library of Congress Cataloging-in-Publication Data

American country cooking. Betty Crocker's American country cooking.

Includes index.   1.   Cookery, American.   I. Crocker, Betty.   II. General Mills, Inc.   III. Title.
TX715.A51252   1987   641.5973   ISBN 0-394-56302-6   87-42642

Manufactured in the United States of America   24689753   First Edition

Contents

Pictured on Page 1: Texas Chili (page 37)

Introduction

Good cooking from many places and backgrounds has contributed to the great variety of recipes from American country kitchens.

A glance through this collection of recipes proves that, even in this great melting pot, the blending of cultures is far from complete. Some of the oldest and simplest American recipe classics are still subject to interpretation. The recipes tell a story about the rich variety of fresh ingredients that were available across this country and also about the ethnic traditions of the immigrants who settled — and continue to settle — in each area.

From this wide array of classics we've chosen a sampler of American favorites that are as appealing today as they were when they originated. And, we have added some current favorites that we think will become the classics in decades to come.

Because America is so large and so heterogeneous, it could never be known for just one way of cooking. The people from all over the world who settled in America brought their own food customs and, often, seeds for these favorite foods in their pockets. In this huge, new country they found a climate or a landscape that reminded them of home. They planted their native seeds, harvested the crops and reproduced their favorite recipes.

What evolved from this beginning was home-grown American cooking characterized by two qualities: legendary ingenuity and a diversity of influences. Few of these recipes would be recognizable today by the settlers' native countrymen. And others, like chili or Crab Louis, although they sound foreign are entirely American innovations. Regardless of influence, country cooking, with its emphasis on fresh, inexpensive, locally available ingredients, has, at its heart, a pride in home and family.

Buffalo Chicken Wings (page 9)

New England and The Middle Atlantic States

It is in New England that some of our most traditional cooking developed as the Pilgrims learned from the Indians how to grow corn, beans, pumpkin and squash. These Indians also introduced the colonists to such native produce as wild blueberries, cranberries, chestnuts and maple syrup.

When colonists began growing grain, they found the land suited for wheat, rye and buckwheat as much as for corn. They grew apples and turned them into uniquely Yankee desserts: deep-dish pies and pandowdies. And, one can hardly think of this region without considering its venerable institutions, clam chowder and the New England Boiled Dinner.

Dutch settlers made the earliest contributions to the cooking of New York. Today a vast diversity of immigrant cooking styles flavors what's eaten in both homes and restaurants throughout the state.

The people known as Pennsylvania Dutch, who came to America from Germany, contributed many recipes to our culinary heritage. One custom still included in their hearty, home-style meals is the practice of serving seven sweet-and-sour relishes with dinner. Those whose settlements encircle Chesapeake Bay have a long-standing love affair with the ample produce of the bay, with Maryland Crab being a particular treasure.

The South

The first cooking traditions of the South were brought from England. For many, the image of this tradition is intertwined with that of large landowners such as George Washington at Mt. Vernon or Thomas Jefferson at Monticello. But in fact, much of the region was settled by farmers who had only small parcels of land.

Because animals and crops thrived in the warm southern climate, corn, sweet potatoes and pork became mainstays of the cooking style. Southern-fried chicken and hot biscuits are distinctly southern traditions, as is fried catfish served with its deep-fried companion, hush puppies. Southerners contributed the recipes we use today for barbecued spareribs and sweet potato pie.

Among the other age-old cooking styles to come from this region are those of New Orleans and the Louisiana bayou country known as Creole and Cajun. Florida's Spanish food heritage today is reinforced by the newer immigrants from the Caribbean. From these shared traditions come two of the South's most enduring qualities, bountiful food and warm hospitality.

Popovers (page 58)

Fruit-stuffed Pork Roast (page 41)

The Midwest and Great Plains

Farming still retains much of its original character in the Midwest and the vast region of the nation's interior from North Dakota to northern Texas called the Great Plains. Hearty, straightforward cooking styles distinguish homesteaders who came not only from older settlements in the East and South but also from the great waves of European immigration at the end of the nineteenth century.

The homesteaders planted corn first, and it flourished in the prairie's newly turned, rich loam soil. When German Mennonites who had been living in the Russian Crimea brought a hardy strain of wheat to Kansas in 1873, they planted the seeds for the miles of waving wheat that are so familiar today. Because so much wheat is now grown in the Great Plains, it is known as the nation's breadbasket.

There is also a Scandinavian character to parts of this region, particularly in Iowa, Wisconsin, Minnesota and the Dakotas. Traditional pork and beef dinners served with mashed potatoes and lots of garden vegetables are examples of the homespun favorites enjoyed in this area. Fish caught in the region's lakes and rivers is often stuffed with America's only native grain, wild rice. It grows wild only in the northern lake country of Minnesota and Wisconsin.

The Southwest

The Southwest is often described by the contrasting cultures by which it is influenced — the American Indian, Spanish, Mexican and Anglo-American. The cooking of the Southwest mirrored these cultures in rich and flavorful combinations. It utilized crops grown by the farming Pueblo Indians and flavors that crossed the border from the northern states of Old Mexico or came to the region with the Spanish missionaries.

Among the foods of the Southwest made popular by the chuck-wagon cooks who fed the cowboys working the vast rangelands are chicken-fried steak and chili. There is a great mystique about chili in Texas — no one agrees to its origin, but it is the most famous Tex-Mex recipe. Tex-Mex cooking developed as American Indian and frontier women adapted Mexican dishes to suit their tastes and the foods they could grow locally.

Outdoor barbecues are popular throughout the Southwest, where long tables groan with sliced meat, corn bread, pinto beans and, what hearty diners in the Southwest consider the indispensable dessert, pecan pie. By all accounts, the eating is hearty and heartfelt in this colorful region.

Cheese Enchiladas (page 32)

Fresh Fruit Tart (page 75)

The Pacific Coast States

Starting in southern California, where Franciscan friars from Spain founded missions as early as some of the East's colonial settlements, a cook's tour of the Pacific Coast ranges northward to the rocky shores of Oregon and Washington, onward to Alaska and across miles of ocean to the island state of Hawaii. There is diversity in both the ethnic history and the food habits of these states, tied together with a ribbon of the blue Pacific.

California is a land that Spanish Mexico once called its own. The culture of the Mexican people is undeniably entrenched throughout California, particularly in the south and along the El Camino Real, where Spanish priests established missions and introduced food of Mexico and Spain to native Indians. Mission gardens held plantings of grapes, avocados and fruit along with corn and beans. The missionaries also introduced chocolate, chilies, tacos and tortillas into California cuisine.

As the gateway to California's gold rush, San Francisco became home to many different people, giving the Golden Gate city an international flavor. Russian, Swiss, Portuguese and Italian immigrants have all influenced the unique flavors of foods in the San Francisco Bay area, but it is in the heart of Chinatown that one feels the cross-cultural influence most.

Oregon attracted Yankee farmers. Germans and Scandinavians settled in Washington. Fruit-tree seedlings that were carried across the Oregon Trail by some of these settlers became the basis for the region's well-known production of apples, pears, Italian "prune" plums, walnuts and filberts.

The Alaskan gold rush brought prospectors carrying not only mining gear but the crocks of sourdough starter to make the pancakes, biscuits and breads for which the entire Northwest is famous.

In marked contrast to Alaska is our fiftieth state, Hawaii. Here a gentle climate encourages a bounty of fresh produce that is available year-round. Hawaii, like the West Coast, enjoys a cultural diversity with Chinese, Filipino and native Hawaiian being the three cultures whose foods lend enticing flavors to some of our favorite outdoor meals.

Appetizers & Light Meals

Buffalo Chicken Wings

Some people have been known to make a meal of chicken wings, and few would dispute their appeal. This appetizing finger food was first served in the Anchor Bar in Buffalo, New York, in 1964. To be *authentic, the peppery hot **wings** — what chicken wings are called in Buffalo — must be served with celery and Blue Cheese dressing.*

Blue Cheese Dressing (right)
2 pounds chicken wings
  Vegetable oil
2 tablespoons margarine or butter, melted
1 tablespoon vinegar
2 to 3 teaspoons red pepper sauce
¼ teaspoon salt
  Celery, carrot or zucchini sticks

Prepare Blue Cheese Dressing; cover and refrigerate at least 3 hours. Cut each chicken wing at joints to make 3 pieces; discard tip. Cut off excess skin; discard.

Heat oil (2 to 3 inches) in deep fryer or Dutch oven to 375°. Fry wings, 4 to 6 at a time, turning occasionally, until golden brown and done, 8 to 10 minutes; drain. Keep warm in 275° oven while frying remaining wings.

Mix margarine, vinegar, pepper sauce and salt in 3-quart bowl until well blended. Add wings; toss until evenly coated with pepper sauce mixture. Serve with Blue Cheese Dressing and celery sticks. *About 24 appetizers.*

Buffalo Chicken Wings, Potato Skins (page 11), Guacamole (page 11)

Blue Cheese Dressing

¾ cup crumbled blue cheese (4 ounces)
1 package (3 ounces) cream cheese, softened
½ cup mayonnaise or salad dressing
⅓ cup half-and-half

Reserve ¼ cup of the blue cheese. Beat remaining blue cheese and the cream cheese on low speed until blended. Add mayonnaise and half-and-half; beat on low speed until creamy. Stir in reserved blue cheese.

Oven-fried Chicken Wings: Omit vegetable oil. Heat 2 tablespoons margarine in rectangular pan, 13 × 9 × 2 inches, in 425° oven until melted. Coat wing pieces with ¼ cup all-purpose flour; shake off excess flour. Arrange wings in pan. Bake uncovered 20 minutes; turn. Bake uncovered until light golden brown, 20 to 25 minutes longer; drain. Decrease margarine in pepper sauce mixture to 1 tablespoon.

Rumaki

*Rumaki — chicken livers and water chestnuts wrapped in bacon — represent just one of the exotic hors d'oeuvres found on the **pupu** platters popular for Hawaiian and West Coast entertaining. Rumaki are Japanese in origin.*

½ pound chicken livers
½ can (8-ounce size) water chestnuts, drained
¼ cup soy sauce
 2 tablespoons packed brown sugar
 2 thin slices gingerroot or ⅛ teaspoon ground
    ginger
 1 clove garlic, crushed
10 slices bacon

Cut chicken livers into halves; cut water chestnuts crosswise into halves. Mix soy sauce, brown sugar, gingerroot and garlic in glass or plastic bowl; stir in chicken livers and water chestnuts. Cover and refrigerate at least 2 hours; drain.

Cut bacon slices into halves. Wrap piece of liver and piece of water chestnut in each bacon piece. Secure with wooden pick. Arrange on rack in broiler pan. Bake uncovered in 400° oven, turning once, until bacon is crisp, 25 to 30 minutes. *20 appetizers.*

Oysters Rockefeller

During the 1800s, the abundant supply of oysters was such that rich and poor alike could enjoy them. Eating a dozen or more at one sitting was standard practice. Among the cities endowed with a plentiful oyster supply was New Orleans. So when the legendary Jules Alciatore of Antoine's restaurant in New Orleans was faced with a shortage of imported snails, he created a number of oyster appetizers as substitutes. His most famous was Oysters Rockefeller. The rich topping — the original recipe is still a family secret — contributed to the recipe being named for one of the turn-of-the-century's richest men, John D. Rockefeller.

   Rock salt
12 medium oysters in shells
 2 tablespoons finely chopped onion
 2 tablespoons snipped parsley
 2 tablespoons finely chopped celery
¼ cup margarine or butter
½ cup chopped fresh or frozen (partially thawed
    and drained) spinach
⅓ cup dry bread crumbs
¼ teaspoon salt
 7 drops red pepper sauce
   Dash of crushed anise seed, if desired

Fill 3 pie plates, 9 × 1¼ inches, ½ inch deep with rock salt; sprinkle with water. Scrub oysters in shells under running cold water. Break off thin end of each shell with hammer. Force a table knife or shucking knife between halves of the shell at broken end; pull apart. Cut oyster at muscle to separate from shell. Remove any bits of shell. Place oyster on deep half of shell; discard other half. Arrange filled shells on rock salt base.

Heat oven to 450°. Cook and stir onion, parsley and celery in margarine until onion is tender. Mix in remaining ingredients. Spoon about 1 tablespoon spinach mixture onto oyster in each shell. Bake 10 minutes. *12 appetizers.*

Potato Skins

Crisply fried potato skins are a relative newcomer in America's snacking repertoire. The oven-baked version is easier and has fewer calories, making it a popular choice among home cooks. Use the pulp that is scooped from inside the potato for hashed browns or potato salad.

---

  6 large baking potatoes
    Guacamole (right)
¼ cup margarine or butter, melted
½ teaspoon salt
½ teaspoon paprika
    Dairy sour cream
    Crisply cooked and crumbled bacon

Bake potatoes in 375° oven until tender, 1 to 1¼ hours. Prepare Guacamole; cover and refrigerate.

Increase oven temperature to 475°. Cut each potato lengthwise into halves. Scoop out potatoes, leaving ¼-inch shell. (Use potatoes as desired.) Brush outsides and insides of shells with margarine. Cut each half lengthwise into halves. Mix salt and paprika; sprinkle over insides of shells. Place shells, cut sides up, on ungreased cookie sheet. Bake uncovered until edges are brown, 15 to 20 minutes. Serve with Guacamole, sour cream and bacon. *24 appetizers.*

To Deep Fry: Bake and scoop out potatoes as directed. Cut each half lengthwise into halves. Heat vegetable oil (2 inches) to 375°. Fry 3 or 4 potato shells at a time until skins are golden brown, 1 to 2 minutes; drain. Sprinkle with salt mixture.

Guacamole

The nutty flavor and buttery texture of a New World native, the avocado, stars in popular dip recipes that range in flavor from fiery to sublime. Most familiar when served with a basket of tortilla chips, guacamole also tops tacos, burritos, enchiladas, potato skins, or is eaten by itself as a salad.

---

  2 very ripe medium avocados, mashed
  1 small onion, finely chopped
  1 green jalapeño chili pepper, finely chopped
  1 tablespoon lemon or lime juice
  1 teaspoon snipped cilantro, if desired
½ teaspoon salt
  1 medium tomato, chopped
    Tortilla chips or Potato skins (left)

Mix avocados, onion, chili, lemon juice, cilantro and salt. Stir in tomato. Cover and refrigerate at least 1 hour. Serve with tortilla chips. *1½ cups dip.*

Salsa Casera

The salsas of Mexico, a word that means sauce in Spanish, brighten the cuisines of the Southwest and West. The fresh-tasting combinations often include tomatoes, onions and jalapeño peppers, lending their colorful character to both dips and condiments.

---

  2 medium tomatoes, finely chopped
  1 medium onion, chopped (about ½ cup)
  1 small clove garlic, finely chopped
  1 canned jalapeño chili pepper, seeded and finely chopped
½ teaspoon jalapeño pepper liquid (from jalapeño pepper can)
  1 tablespoon finely snipped cilantro, if desired
  1 tablespoon lemon juice
1½ teaspoons vegetable oil
½ teaspoon dried oregano leaves

Mix all ingredients. Cover and refrigerate in glass or plastic container no longer than 1 week. *About 2 cups sauce.*

New England Clam Chowder

*References to clam chowders appear in the early "receipt" books of New England. Fish and seafood stews — simple preparations of the day's catch seasoned with salt pork and milk — were a custom brought to Canada by French fishermen. To make the stew, they used a large pot known as **la chaudière**. As the stew became popular along the New England coast, the name of the pot became the name for the stew — what we know as chowder.*

Potatoes were added to chowder only after they became generally available in the 1800s. Before that, chowders were thickened with pilot crackers, a version of a ship's biscuits or hardtack. Pilot or oyster crackers are still a popular accompaniment for this most American of seafood stews.

¼ cup cut-up bacon or lean salt pork
1 medium onion, chopped (about ½ cup)
2 cans (8 ounces each) minced clams, drained (reserve liquid)
2 medium potatoes, diced
  Dash of pepper
2 cups milk

Cook and stir bacon and onion in 2-quart saucepan until bacon is crisp. Add enough water, if necessary, to reserved clam liquid to measure 1 cup. Stir clams, liquid, potatoes and pepper into onion mixture. Heat to boiling; reduce heat. Cover and boil until potatoes are tender, about 15 minutes. Stir in milk. Heat, stirring occasionally, just until hot (do not boil). *4 servings.*

New Hampshire Cheese Soup

What an old-timer would call store or rat cheese, the staple kind of aged Cheddar that was found in every farmhouse, country store or corner grocery, lends its robust flavor to this vegetable soup recipe.

---

1 large potato, finely chopped
1 large onion, finely chopped
¼ cup chopped carrots
¼ cup thinly sliced celery
1 cup water
1 cup shredded sharp Cheddar cheese (4 ounces)
2 cups chicken broth
½ cup half-and-half
2 tablespoons snipped parsley

Heat vegetables and water to boiling in 2-quart saucepan; reduce heat. Cover and simmer until vegetables are tender, 10 to 15 minutes. Stir in cheese, broth and half-and-half; heat through. Sprinkle with parsley. *4 to 6 servings.*

Senate Bean Soup

Senate Bean Soup is served every day in the restaurant of the United States Senate.

---

1 pound dried navy beans (about 2 cups)
12 cups water
1 ham bone
2½ cups mashed cooked potatoes
2 teaspoons salt
¼ teaspoon pepper
1 large onion, chopped (about 1 cup)
2 stalks celery, chopped
1 clove garlic, finely chopped

Heat beans and water to boiling in Dutch oven. Boil 2 minutes; remove from heat. Cover and let stand 1 hour.

Add ham bone. Heat to boiling; reduce heat. Cover and simmer until beans are tender, about 2 hours. Stir in remaining ingredients. Cover and simmer 1 hour. Remove ham bone; trim ham from bone and stir into soup. *12 to 14 servings.*

Wild Rice Soup

Wild Rice Soup

Minnesota cooks have experimented with any number of recipes using their indigenous delicacy, *wild rice. Creamy chowder-like soups are among the most popular results.*

---

2 medium stalks celery, sliced
1 medium carrot, coarsely shredded
1 medium onion, chopped (about ½ cup)
1 small green pepper, chopped
2 tablespoons margarine or butter
3 tablespoons all-purpose flour
1 teaspoon salt
¼ teaspoon pepper
1½ cups cooked wild rice
1 cup water
1 can (10¾ ounces) condensed chicken broth
1 cup half-and-half
⅓ cup slivered almonds, toasted
¼ cup snipped parsley

Cook and stir celery, carrot, onion and green pepper in margarine in 3-quart saucepan until celery is tender, about 5 minutes. Stir in flour, salt and pepper. Stir in wild rice, water and broth. Heat to boiling; reduce heat. Cover and simmer 15 minutes, stirring occasionally. Stir in remaining ingredients. Heat just until hot (do not boil). *5 servings.*

Classic Cornish Pasties

Immigrants, known by the nicknames Cousin Jack and Cousin Jenny, from the mining region of Cornwall, England who came to work the mines of Minnesota, Wisconsin and Michigan's Upper Peninsula brought the tradition of encasing meat, potatoes and vegetables in a pastry crust. The miners' wives baked these large sustaining turnovers into portable lunches for men who often spent up to fourteen hours in the mines. The pasties can be eaten hot or cold, out of hand or on a plate, making them appealing for picnics and suppers.

Pastry (right)
1 medium potato, diced (about 1 cup)
¾ pound beef boneless round or chuck steak, cut into ¼-inch pieces
2 medium carrots, diced (about 1 cup)
1 medium onion, chopped (about ½ cup)
½ small turnip or rutabaga, diced (about ½ cup)
 Salt and pepper
6 teaspoons margarine or butter
6 teaspoons water
 Flour
 Milk
 Corn Relish (page 64), pickled beets, chili sauce or pickles

Arrange oven racks to divide oven evenly into thirds. Heat oven to 350°.

Prepare Pastry. Place 3 pastry circles on each of 2 ungreased large cookie sheets. Layer potato, beef, carrots, onion and turnip on half of each circle to within 1½ inches of edge. Sprinkle with salt and pepper. Dot with 1 teaspoon margarine and sprinkle with 1 teaspoon water.

Brush edge of each circle with water. Fold plain half of circle over filling; fold edges up and seal with fork dipped in flour. Cut small slits in top; brush lightly with milk.

Bake 30 minutes; reverse cookie sheets on oven racks. Bake 30 minutes longer. Serve with Corn Relish. *6 servings.*

Pastry

2⅔ cups all-purpose flour
1 teaspoon salt
1 cup shortening
7 to 8 tablespoons cold water

Mix flour and salt. Cut in shortening until particles are size of small peas. Sprinkle in water, 1 tablespoon at a time, tossing with fork until all flour is moistened and pastry almost cleans side of bowl (1 to 2 teaspoons water can be added if necessary).

Gather pastry into ball; divide into 6 equal parts on lightly floured cloth-covered board. Roll each part into 9-inch circle with lightly floured cloth-covered rolling pin.

Philly Beef Sandwiches

The appeal of Philadelphia's cheese-steak sandwich has led to its introduction across America in recent years. Our version combines thin slices of cooked beef roast, grilled onions and the traditional melted cheese. In Philadelphia's Italian market neighborhood, birthplace of the sandwich in the 1930s, cheese-steak toppings can also include grilled mushrooms and peppers, tomato and hot sauces.

---

 2 medium onions, sliced
 2 tablespoons margarine or butter
 6 hoagie or frankfurter buns, split and toasted
 1¼ pounds thinly sliced cooked beef roast
 12 slices process American cheese

Cook and stir onions in margarine until tender, about 10 minutes. Set oven control to broil. Place bottom halves of buns on ungreased cookie sheet; top with onions and beef. Cut cheese slices into halves; place 4 halves on each sandwich. Broil with tops 5 to 6 inches from heat just until cheese is melted, 2 to 3 minutes. Top each with remaining bun half. *6 sandwiches.*

Sloppy Joes

One of America's favorite quick lunches, that's been enjoyed by generations of school children.

---

 1 pound ground beef
 1 medium onion, chopped (about ½ cup)
 ⅓ cup chopped celery
 ⅓ cup chopped green pepper
 ⅓ cup catsup
 ¼ cup water
 1 tablespoon Worcestershire sauce
 ½ teaspoon salt
 ⅛ teaspoon red pepper sauce
 6 hamburger buns, split and toasted

Cook and stir ground beef and onion in 10-inch skillet until beef is brown; drain. Stir in remaining ingredients except buns. Cover and cook over low heat just until vegetables are tender, 10 to 15 minutes. Fill buns with beef mixture. *6 sandwiches.*

Reuben Sandwiches

As many variations exist for this popular sandwich as those who claim its origin. New Yorkers are sure to credit its origin to the now-closed deli, Reuben's, where towering sandwich creations in the 1940s and 1950s often named celebrities in the titles. Nebraskans swear that Reuben Kay, an Omaha wholesale grocer, came up with the sandwich to serve at a card game. The first winner of the National Sandwich Idea Contest in 1956 was none other than the Reuben. Whether served open-faced, with melted cheese or grilled (as is the case with our rendition), Reuben advocates agree on one thing — the accompaniment of mustard and pickles.

 ⅓ cup mayonnaise or salad dressing
 1 tablespoon chili sauce
 12 slices rye bread
 6 slices Swiss cheese
 ¾ pound thinly sliced cooked corned beef
 1 can (16 ounces) sauerkraut, drained
      Margarine or butter, softened

Mix mayonnaise and chili sauce; spread over 6 slices bread. Arrange cheese, corned beef and sauerkraut on mayonnaise mixture; top with remaining bread slices. Spread top slices of bread with margarine. Place sandwiches, margarine sides down, in skillet. Spread tops of bread with margarine. Cook uncovered over low heat until bottoms are golden brown, about 10 minutes. Turn; cook until golden brown and cheese is melted, about 8 minutes longer. *6 sandwiches.*

Rachel Sandwiches: Substitute 1½ cups Coleslaw (page 47) for the sauerkraut and thinly sliced cooked turkey or chicken for half of the corned beef.

Seafood Salad in Pita

Coastal regions, with their abundance of fresh shell-fish, are known for sandwiches heaped with chunks of crabmeat, shrimp and lobster lightly dressed with mayonnaise. Pita breads often hold the West Coast variations, while in Maine and Massachusetts hot dog rolls are filled to make the renowned lobster roll.

1/2 cup mayonnaise or salad dressing
 1 tablespoon finely chopped green onion (with top)
1/2 teaspoon salt
   Dash of pepper
 2 cups cut-up cooked shrimp or crabmeat or 1 package (8 ounces) frozen salad-style imitation crabmeat, thawed*
 2 cups thinly sliced celery
 4 pita breads (6-inch diameter)
   Tomato slices
   Alfalfa sprouts

Mix mayonnaise, onion, salt and pepper; toss with shrimp and celery. Cover tightly and refrigerate at least 2 hours. Cut pita breads crosswise into halves. Fill each half with about 1/2 cup shrimp mixture. Insert tomato slices and alfalfa sprouts in each. *8 sandwiches.*

*Two packages (6 ounces each) frozen cooked crabmeat, thawed, or 2 cans (6 1/2 ounces each) crabmeat, drained and cartilage removed, can be substituted for the fresh or imitation crabmeat.

Lobster Rolls: Substitute cut-up cooked lobster for the shrimp and 8 hot dog rolls or frankfurter buns, toasted, for the pita breads. Omit tomatoes and alfalfa sprouts.

Muffuletta

The Muffuletta is a monumental sandwich creation which boasts an unusual combination of ingredients layered between halves of chewy Italian bread loaves known by the same muffuletta name. What distinguishes this New Orleans specialty from its cousin, the Italian hero, is Olive Salad, a pungent pickled vegetable mixture that garnishes the cold-cut filling. The Central Grocery in New Orleans claims the original Muffuletta, and still serves it today.

   Olive Salad (below)
 1 unsliced large round or oval loaf Italian or sourdough bread (8- to 10-inch diameter)
1/2 pound thinly sliced Italian salami
1/3 pound thinly sliced provolone cheese
1/4 pound thinly sliced fully cooked smoked ham

Prepare Olive Salad. Cut bread horizontally into halves. Remove 1/2-inch layer of soft bread from inside of each half to within 1/2 inch of edge. Drain Olive Salad, reserving marinade. Brush reserved marinade over cut sides of bread. Layer salami, 1/2 of the Olive Salad, the cheese, ham and remaining Olive Salad on bottom half of bread. Cover with top half of bread. *6 servings.*

Olive Salad

 1 anchovy fillet, mashed
 1 large clove garlic, crushed
1/3 cup olive oil
1/2 cup chopped pimiento-stuffed olives
1/2 cup chopped Greek or ripe olives
1/2 cup chopped mixed pickled vegetables
 2 tablespoons snipped parsley
1/2 teaspoon dried oregano leaves, crushed
1/8 teaspoon pepper

Stir anchovy and garlic into oil in 1-quart glass or plastic bowl until well blended. Stir in remaining ingredients. Cover and marinate in refrigerator at least 8 hours, stirring occasionally.

Muffuletta

Cobb Salad

Tracing its origin to Hollywood's Brown Derby restaurant, Cobb Salad is but one of America's salad favorites from California. Salad ingredients, similar to those in the club sandwich, are arranged in colorful rows, then served with tangy Lemon Vinaigrette.

Lemon Vinaigrette (right)
6 cups finely shredded lettuce
2 cups cut-up cooked chicken
3 hard-cooked eggs, chopped
2 medium tomatoes, chopped
1 ripe avocado, chopped
¼ cup crumbled blue cheese (1 ounce)
4 slices bacon, crisply cooked and crumbled

Prepare Lemon Vinaigrette. Divide salad greens among 4 individual salad plates or in salad bowls. Arrange remaining ingredients on lettuce. Serve with vinaigrette. *4 servings.*

Lemon Vinaigrette

½ cup vegetable oil
¼ cup lemon juice
1 tablespoon red wine vinegar
2 teaspoons sugar
½ teaspoon dry mustard
½ teaspoon salt
½ teaspoon Worcestershire sauce
¼ teaspoon garlic powder
¼ teaspoon pepper

Shake all ingredients in tightly covered container. Refrigerate at least 1 hour.

Cobb Salad

Taco Salads

One of America's recent popular salad meals takes the Mexican snacktime specialty, tacos, and adds a new dimension by making a bowl from the tortilla. Tacos themselves became known to Americans only after the 1930s.

Tortilla Shells (below)
1 pound ground beef
²/₃ cup water
1 tablespoon chili powder
1½ teaspoons salt
¼ teaspoon garlic powder
¼ teaspoon ground red pepper
1 can (15½ ounces) kidney beans, drained
   (reserve empty can)
1 medium head lettuce, torn into bite-size pieces
   (about 10 cups)
1 cup shredded Cheddar cheese (4 ounces)
²/₃ cup sliced ripe olives
2 medium tomatoes, coarsely chopped
1 medium onion, chopped (about ½ cup)
¾ cup Thousand Island dressing
1 avocado, thinly sliced
   Dairy sour cream

Prepare Tortilla Shells. Cook and stir ground beef in 10-inch skillet until brown; drain. Stir in water, chili powder, salt, garlic powder, red pepper and beans. Heat to boiling; reduce heat. Simmer uncovered 15 minutes, stirring occasionally; cool 10 minutes.

Mix lettuce, cheese, olives, tomatoes and onion in 3-quart bowl; toss with dressing. Pour beef mixture on top; toss. Divide among Tortilla Shells; garnish with avocado and sour cream. Serve immediately. *8 servings.*

Tortilla Shells

Remove label and both ends of kidney bean can; wash and dry. Heat vegetable oil (1½ inches) in 3-quart saucepan to 375°. (Diameter of saucepan should be no wider than 9 inches.) Place 1 of 8 flour tortillas (10-inch diameter) on top of saucepan; place can on center of tortilla with long-handled tongs. Push tortilla into oil by gently pushing can down. Fry tortilla until slightly set, about 5 seconds; remove

can with tongs. Continue frying tortilla, turning in oil, until crisp and golden brown, 1 to 2 minutes longer. Carefully remove tortilla from oil; drain excess oil from inside. Turn tortilla shell upside down; cool. Repeat with remaining tortillas. (Cooled Tortilla Shells can be covered tightly and stored at room temperature no longer than 24 hours.)

Crab Louis

Generous supplies of succulent Dungeness and king crab were reason enough for West Coast restaurateurs to come up with this salad classic. It has a French-sounding name for no reason at all. The chili sauce in the dressing was a brand-new American convenience product in 1914, making the distinctive pink-hued Louis Dressing possible.

---

4 cups bite-size pieces salad greens
2 cups cut-up cooked crabmeat or 1 package (8
   ounces) frozen salad-style imitation crabmeat,
   thawed
4 tomatoes, cut into fourths
4 hard-cooked eggs, cut into fourths
   Ripe or pimiento-stuffed olives
   Louis Dressing (below)

Divide salad greens among 4 large individual salad bowls or plates. Arrange crabmeat, tomatoes, eggs and olives on lettuce. Pour Louis Dressing over salads. *4 servings.*

Louis Dressing

¾ cup chili sauce
½ cup mayonnaise or salad dressing
1 teaspoon finely chopped onion
½ teaspoon sugar
¼ teaspoon Worcestershire sauce
   Salt to taste

Mix all ingredients; refrigerate 30 minutes.

Main Dishes

Baked Salmon Steaks

Salmon caught in the cold, clear waters off the Alaska coast are one of the best-known products of our forty-ninth state. The species of salmon most available for cooking fresh are the King (Chinook) and Silver (Coho) salmon. Simple preparations, like this one inspired by salmon eaten when on a vacation in the Northwest, are something special.

---

    2 tablespoons lemon juice
    ¼ cup packed brown sugar
    4 salmon steaks, 1 inch thick (about 2 pounds)
    1 tablespoon margarine or butter, melted
    4 thin slices lemon
    8 teaspoons brown sugar

Heat oven to 375°. Pour lemon juice into ungreased rectangular baking dish, 11 × 7½ × 2 inches; sprinkle with ¼ cup brown sugar. Arrange salmon steaks in dish; drizzle with margarine. Bake uncovered 15 minutes; turn. Place 1 slice lemon on each salmon steak; sprinkle with 2 teaspoons brown sugar. Bake until fish flakes easily with fork, 15 to 20 minutes longer. Serve with juices from dish. *4 servings.*

Smoked Salmon

Salmon smoked with hickory chips on a backyard grill harkens to the traditions of Northwest Coast Indians who skewered salmon on alderwood sticks to roast over blazing wood fires.

    3 cups hickory wood chips
    2 tablespoons margarine or butter, melted
    2 tablespoons lemon juice
    2 tablespoons snipped fresh dill weed or 1 teaspoon
       dried dill weed
      3-pound salmon, cleaned

Cover hickory chips with water. Let stand 30 minutes; drain.

Mix margarine, lemon juice and dill weed; brush on both sides of salmon. Add 1 cup hickory chips to hot charcoal. Fill water pan with water. Place salmon on rack about 6 inches from water pan over coals. Cover smoker and smoke-cook salmon, brushing once or twice with lemon juice mixture, until salmon flakes easily with fork (180°), 3 to 4 hours. Add charcoal and soaked hickory chips every hour (add water to pan during cooking if necessary).

Cut salmon into serving pieces. Garnish with fresh dill weed and lemon slices if desired. *16 servings.*

Baked Salmon Steaks, West Coast Orange Salad (page 50)

Wild Rice-stuffed Northern Pike

*The Indians of Minnesota and Wisconsin's northern lake country have long revered the tall aquatic grasses called **mahnomen** — wild rice. This nutty brown grain has a slightly smoky taste, making it a favorite accompaniment to one of the Indians' favorite game fish, the northern pike.*

2½- to 3-pound northern pike, cleaned
Wild Rice Stuffing (below)
Lemon juice
Salt
Vegetable oil
¼ cup margarine or butter, melted
2 tablespoons lemon juice
Lemon wedges

Prepare Wild Rice Stuffing. Rub cavity of pike with lemon juice; sprinkle with salt. Loosely stuff with Wild Rice Stuffing. Close opening with skewers and lace with string. (Spoon any remaining stuffing into buttered baking dish; cover and refrigerate. Place in oven with pike 30 minutes before pike is done.)

Brush pike with oil; place in shallow roasting pan. Mix margarine and 2 tablespoons lemon juice. Bake pike uncovered in 350° oven, brushing occasionally with margarine mixture, until pike flakes easily with fork, 50 to 60 minutes. Serve with lemon wedges. *6 servings.*

Wild Rice Stuffing

¾ cup uncooked wild rice
2 cups water
1½ teaspoons instant chicken bouillon
½ cup thinly sliced celery
½ cup chopped onion
¼ cup slivered almonds
¼ cup margarine or butter
8 ounces mushrooms, sliced (about 2½ cups)

Heat rice, water and bouillon to boiling, stirring once or twice; reduce heat. Cover and simmer until tender, 40 to 50 minutes. After cooking rice 30 minutes, check to see that rice is not sticking to pan. Add 2 to 3 tablespoons water if necessary.

Cook and stir celery, onion and almonds in margarine in 10-inch skillet over medium heat until vegetables are tender and almonds are light brown. Add mushrooms; cook until tender, about 5 minutes longer. Stir in wild rice.

Smoked Salmon and Scalloped Potatoes

Creamy scalloped potatoes teamed with bits of smoked salmon probably has its origin among those settlers in the Northwest who came from New England. In that region combinations of potatoes and North Atlantic cod were popular mainstays for family dinners.

---

3 tablespoons margarine or butter
3 tablespoons all-purpose flour
½ teaspoon salt
¼ teaspoon pepper
2½ cups milk
2 tablespoons snipped parsley
2 pounds potatoes (about 6 medium), thinly sliced (about 4 cups)
1 small onion, finely chopped (about ¼ cup)
¾ pound flaked boned smoked salmon
1 tablespoon margarine or butter

Heat 3 tablespoons margarine in 1½-quart saucepan over low heat until melted. Stir in flour, salt and pepper. Cook over low heat, stirring constantly, until smooth and bubbly; remove from heat. Stir in milk. Heat to boiling, stirring constantly. Boil and stir 1 minute. Stir in parsley.

Layer ⅓ of the potatoes, ½ of the onion and salmon and ⅓ of the white sauce in greased 2-quart casserole; repeat. Top with remaining potatoes and sauce. Dot with 1 tablespoon margarine. Cover and bake in 350° oven 30 minutes. Uncover and bake until potatoes are tender, 60 to 70 minutes longer. Let stand 5 to 10 minutes before serving. *6 servings.*

Ham and Scalloped Potatoes: Substitute 1½ cups cubed fully cooked smoked ham for the salmon. Omit parsley.

Pompano en Papillote

Pompano is a delicate-flavored whitefish found in the warm waters of the Gulf of Mexico. Pompano en Papillote is another of the renowned foods that originated in the kitchen of Antoine's restaurant in New Orleans. Wanting to honor visiting French balloonist Alberto Santos-Dumont, Antoine's chef sealed fish fillets, mushroom sauce and shrimp in parchment bags that dramatically puffed during baking to resemble a turn-of-the-century balloon. It's customary to open the papillotes in front of guests so they can savor the aroma of this Creole classic.

Pompano en Papillote

2 cups water
½ cup dry white wine
½ teaspoon salt
1 medium onion, sliced
3 slices lemon
3 sprigs parsley
1 bay leaf
4 peppercorns
1 pound pompano fillets, cut into 4 equal pieces*
  Mushroom Sauce (right)
4 pieces kitchen parchment paper or aluminum foil, 12 × 15 inches
  Vegetable oil
12 cleaned medium raw shrimp (about 1 cup)

Heat water, wine, salt, onion, lemon, parsley, bay leaf and peppercorns to boiling in 12-inch skillet; reduce heat. Cover and simmer 5 minutes. Place pompano fillets in skillet. Heat to boiling; reduce heat. Simmer uncovered until fish flakes easily with fork, 3 to 6 minutes. Carefully remove fish with slotted spoon; drain on wire rack. Reserve cooking liquid in skillet.

Heat oven to 400°. Prepare Mushroom Sauce. Cut each piece of parchment paper into heart shape, about 12 inches long by 14 inches wide. Brush oil on top of each heart to within ½ inch of edge.

Spoon ¼ cup Mushroom Sauce onto half of each heart. Place 1 piece of fish on sauce. Arrange 3 shrimp on fish; spoon about 1 tablespoon sauce over shrimp. Fold other half of heart over top. Beginning at top of heart, seal edges by turning up and folding together; twist tip of heart to hold packet closed. Bake on ungreased cookie sheet until paper puffs up and is light brown, about 15 minutes. To serve, cut a large X shape on top of each packet; fold back corners. *4 servings.*

Trout, pike, halibut, haddock or orange roughy fillets can be substituted for the pompano fillets.

Mushroom Sauce

  Reserved cooking liquid
1 cup sliced mushrooms
3 tablespoons margarine or butter
3 tablespoons all-purpose flour
¼ teaspoon salt
⅛ teaspoon white pepper
¼ cup half-and-half

Strain reserved cooking liquid. Heat to boiling; continue boiling until liquid measures 1 cup. Cook mushrooms and margarine in 1½ quart saucepan over low heat, stirring occasionally, until mushrooms are tender, about 5 minutes. Stir in flour, salt and pepper. Cook over low heat, stirring constantly, until smooth and bubbly; remove from heat. Gradually stir in liquid and half-and-half. Heat to boiling, stirring constantly. Boil and stir 1 minute.

Southern-fried Catfish

A favorite along the Mississippi valley from Iowa to Louisiana, fresh catfish fried in a peppery cornmeal crust is the focal point of local fish fries. Hush puppies and coleslaw are an inseparable part of the menu for these gatherings.

    Vegetable oil
1¼ cups cornmeal
  1 teaspoon salt
  ½ teaspoon ground red pepper
  ¼ teaspoon pepper
  6 small catfish (about ½ pound each), skinned
     and pan-dressed
  ½ cup all-purpose flour
  2 eggs, slightly beaten

Heat oil (½ inch) in 12-inch skillet over medium-high heat until hot. Mix cornmeal, salt, red pepper and pepper; reserve. Coat catfish with flour; dip into eggs. Coat with cornmeal mixture. Fry catfish, 2 at a time, until golden brown, about 6 minutes on each side. Keep warm in 275° oven while frying remaining catfish. *6 servings.*

Maryland Crab Cakes

Cooking on Maryland's eastern shore is synonymous with seafood. Local cooks insist on using Atlantic crabmeat, the lightest seasoning and gentle handling for an authentic taste. Accompany Maryland Crab Cakes with tartar sauce.

---

  1 pound cooked Atlantic crabmeat, cartilage
     removed and flaked (2½ to 3 cups)
1½ cups soft white bread crumbs (without crusts)
  2 tablespoons margarine or butter, melted
  1 teaspoon dry mustard
  ½ teaspoon salt
  ⅛ teaspoon pepper
  2 egg yolks, beaten
    Vegetable oil

Mix all ingredients except oil. Shape into 4 patties. Refrigerate until firm. Heat oil (1 inch) to 375°. Fry patties until golden brown on both sides, 4 to 5 minutes; drain. *4 servings.*

Shrimp Creole

Shrimp Creole is a Louisiana classic that boasts remarkably easy preparation. Shrimp specialties evolved among the Creole population, descendants of the early Spanish and French families, because shrimp was abundant and could be prepared in many delicious ways. Remember that shrimp cook in only a few minutes; longer cooking makes them tough.

---

  2 pounds fresh or frozen raw shrimp (in shells)
1½ cups chopped onion
  1 cup finely chopped celery
  2 medium green peppers, finely chopped
  2 cloves garlic, finely chopped
  ¼ cup margarine or butter
  1 cup water
  2 teaspoons snipped parsley
  1 teaspoon salt
  ⅛ teaspoon ground red pepper
  2 bay leaves
  1 can (15 ounces) tomato sauce
  3 cups hot cooked rice

Peel shrimp. (If shrimp are frozen, do not thaw; peel under running cold water.) Make a shallow cut lengthwise down back of each shrimp; wash out sand vein. Cover and refrigerate.

Cook and stir onion, celery, green peppers and garlic in margarine in 3-quart saucepan until onion is tender. Stir in water, parsley, salt, red pepper, bay leaves and tomato sauce. Heat to boiling; reduce heat. Simmer uncovered 10 minutes.

Stir in shrimp. Heat to boiling. Cover and cook over medium heat until shrimp are pink, 10 to 20 minutes. Remove bay leaves. Serve over rice. *6 servings.*

Shrimp Etouffée

*Another of Louisiana's famous foods is the hearty, highly peppered stew called **étouffée**. It is made with shrimp or the Cajun specialty, crawfish, that are smothered — what **étouffée** means in French — while they cook with flavorful vegetables. If you, like a Louisiana Cajun, prefer more "heat," add red pepper sauce a little at a time until the flavor suits your taste.*

---

1 pound fresh or frozen medium raw shrimp
   (in shells)
¼ cup margarine or butter
2 tablespoons all-purpose flour
1 medium onion, chopped (about ½ cup)
1 small green pepper, chopped (about ½ cup)
1 medium stalk celery, sliced (about ½ cup)
1 clove garlic, finely chopped
1 cup water
2 tablespoons snipped parsley
2 teaspoons lemon juice
½ teaspoon salt
¼ teaspoon pepper
⅛ to ¼ teaspoon red pepper sauce
   Hot cooked rice

Peel shrimp. (If shrimp are frozen, do not thaw; peel under running cold water.) Make a shallow cut lengthwise down back of each shrimp; wash out sand vein. Heat margarine in 3-quart saucepan over medium-low heat until melted. Stir in flour. Cook, stirring constantly, until bubbly and brown, about 6 minutes. Stir in onion, green pepper, celery and garlic. Cook and stir until vegetables are crisp-tender, about 5 minutes.

Stir in shrimp, water, parsley, lemon juice, salt, pepper and pepper sauce. Heat to boiling; reduce heat. Simmer uncovered, stirring occasionally, until shrimp are pink, about 5 minutes. Serve over rice. *4 servings.*

Crawfish Etouffée: Substitute cleaned raw crawfish for the shrimp. (Sizes of crawfish vary depending on region and variety. Forty to forty-eight crawfish, each about 5 inches long, yield about 1 pound tail meat.)

Shrimp Etouffée

Turkey with Chestnut Stuffing

American chestnut trees were once a familiar sight, growing in forests from Maine to Alabama. When nearly all the trees were killed by the great chestnut blight in 1904, Americans looked to southern Europe for a supply of these shiny brown nuts. Fresh chestnuts can usually be found in American markets at Thanksgiving time to lend their distinctive flavor to holiday turkeys.

Chestnut Stuffing (right)
10- to 12-pound turkey
Margarine or butter, melted

Prepare Chestnut Stuffing. Fill wishbone area with stuffing. Fasten neck skin to back with skewer. Fold wings across back with tips touching. Fill body cavity lightly. (Do not pack — stuffing will expand.) Tuck drumsticks under band of skin at tail or skewer to tail.

Place turkey, breast side up, on rack in shallow roasting pan. Brush with margarine. Insert meat thermometer so tip is in thickest part of inside thigh muscle or thickest part of breast meat and does not touch bone. (Tip of thermometer can be inserted in center of stuffing.) Do not add water. Do not cover. Roast in 325° oven until done, 3½ to 4 hours.

Place a tent of aluminum foil loosely over turkey when it begins to turn golden. When ⅔ done, cut band or remove skewer holding legs. Turkey is done when thermometer placed in thigh muscle registers 185° or drumstick meat feels very soft. (Thermometer inserted in stuffing will register 165°.)

Let stand about 20 minutes before carving. As soon as possible after serving, remove every bit of stuffing from turkey. Cool stuffing and turkey promptly; refrigerate separately and use within 2 days. *8 to 10 servings.*

Chestnut Stuffing

```
    1  pound chestnuts
 1½  cups chopped celery (with leaves)
  ¾  cup finely chopped onion
    1  cup margarine or butter
    7  cups soft bread cubes
    2  teaspoons salt
 1½  teaspoons dried sage leaves
    1  teaspoon dried thyme leaves
  ½  teaspoon pepper
```

Cut X shape on rounded side of each chestnut. Heat chestnuts and enough water to cover to boiling. Boil uncovered 10 minutes; drain. Remove shells and skins. Heat chestnuts and enough water to cover to boiling. Boil uncovered 10 minutes; drain and chop.

Cook and stir celery, onion and margarine in 10-inch skillet until onion is tender. Stir in about ⅓ of the bread cubes. Turn mixture into deep bowl. Add remaining bread cubes, the salt, sage, thyme, pepper and chestnuts; toss.

Turkey with Corn Bread Stuffing: Omit chestnuts. Substitute 9 cups corn bread cubes for the soft bread cubes.

Turkey with Oyster Stuffing: Omit chestnuts. Increase bread cubes to 8 cups and add 2 cans (8 ounces each) oysters, drained and chopped.

Southern-fried Chicken

This Deep South favorite is an American classic that has never gone out of style. Although southern cooks may disagree on the method to use for frying chicken, all agree that it should be served with Creamy Gravy.

½ cup all-purpose flour
1 teaspoon salt
1 teaspoon paprika
¼ teaspoon pepper
   2½- to 3-pound broiler-fryer chicken, cut up
   Vegetable oil
   Creamy Gravy (below)

Mix flour, salt, paprika and pepper. Coat chicken with flour mixture. Heat oil (¼ inch) in 12-inch skillet over medium-high heat until hot. Cook chicken in oil until light brown on all sides, about 10 minutes; reduce heat. Cover tightly and simmer, turning once or twice, until thickest pieces are done, about 35 minutes. (If skillet cannot be covered tightly, add 1 to 2 tablespoons water.) Remove cover during last 5 minutes of cooking to crisp chicken. Remove chicken; keep warm. Prepare Creamy Gravy; serve with chicken. *6 servings.*

Creamy Gravy

2 tablespoons all-purpose flour
½ cup chicken broth or water
½ cup milk
   Salt and pepper to taste

Pour drippings from skillet into bowl, leaving brown particles in skillet. Return 2 tablespoons drippings to skillet. Stir in flour. Cook over low heat, stirring constantly, until smooth and bubbly; remove from heat. Stir in broth and milk. Heat to boiling, stirring constantly. Boil and stir 1 minute. Stir in a few drops browning sauce if desired. Stir in salt and pepper.

Maryland-fried Chicken: Coat chicken with flour mixture. Beat 2 eggs and 2 tablespoons water. Dip flour-coated chicken into egg mixture; coat chicken with 2 cups soda cracker crumbs, dry bread crumbs or 1 cup cornmeal mixed with ½ teaspoon salt. Omit Creamy Gravy.

Chicken in Cream

The politician who promises a chicken in every pot will probably get the votes, for chicken always has been an unequivocal winner. From Maine to Hawaii, there are innumerable recipes for preparing this versatile bird. Chicken in Cream has attributes busy cooks appreciate: it's distinctive and requires little watching.

½ cup all-purpose flour
1 teaspoon salt
¼ teaspoon pepper
   2½- to 3-pound broiler-fryer chicken, cut up
2 cups half-and-half
   Paprika

Mix flour, salt and pepper. Coat chicken with flour mixture. Place chicken, skin sides down, in ungreased rectangular baking dish, 13 × 9 × 2 inches. Pour half-and-half over chicken. Bake uncovered in 325° oven 45 minutes; turn chicken. Bake uncovered until thickest pieces are done, 30 to 45 minutes longer (do not overbake). Remove chicken; keep warm. Stir enough hot water or milk into baking dish, if necessary, until sauce is desired consistency; pour over chicken. Sprinkle with paprika. *6 servings.*

Hawaiian-style Chicken

Hawaii's cuisine reflects the heritage of the native Polynesians along with the Japanese, Chinese, Korean, Spanish, Filipino, Portuguese and mainland American people who came to the islands.

---

1 tablespoon vegetable oil
⅓ cup frozen (thawed) orange juice concentrate
1 egg, slightly beaten
⅓ cup all-purpose flour
1 teaspoon ground ginger
1 teaspoon salt
   2½- to 3-pound broiler-fryer chicken, cut up
   About 2 cups shredded coconut
2 tablespoons margarine or butter, melted

Spread oil on bottom of rectangular pan, 13 × 9 × 2 inches. Mix orange juice concentrate and egg; reserve. Mix flour, ginger and salt. Coat chicken with flour mixture. Dip chicken into orange juice mixture, then coat with coconut.

Place chicken, skin sides up, in pan. Drizzle with margarine. Bake uncovered in 375°oven until thickest pieces are done, 60 to 70 minutes. If necessary, cover lightly with aluminum foil during last 15 minutes of baking to prevent excessive browning. *6 servings.*

Chicken Breasts Teriyaki

The Japanese inhabitants of Hawaii introduced the now universally popular teriyaki flavor used for grilled chicken, fish and beef.

¼ cup soy sauce
¼ cup sweet white wine
1 tablespoon sugar
1 tablespoon vegetable oil
1 teaspoon crushed gingerroot or ¼ teaspoon
   ground ginger
1 clove garlic, crushed
2 whole chicken breasts (about 1½ pounds), boned,
   skinned and cut into halves

Mix all ingredients except chicken breasts; pour over chicken. Cover and refrigerate at least 1 hour.

Remove chicken; reserve marinade. Cover and grill chicken 5 to 6 inches from medium coals until golden brown, about 15 minutes; turn chicken. Cover and grill, turning and brushing 2 or 3 times with marinade, until chicken is done, 10 to 20 minutes longer. *4 servings.*

Arroz con Pollo

A strong Spanish influence is evident in this colorful recipe for chicken with rice. It is equally popular among Americans of Caribbean and Mexican heritage.

   2½- to 3-pound broiler-fryer chicken, cut up
¾ teaspoon salt
¼ to ½ teaspoon paprika
¼ teaspoon pepper
2½ cups chicken broth
1 cup uncooked regular rice
1 medium onion, chopped
1 teaspoon garlic salt
½ teaspoon dried oregano leaves
⅛ teaspoon ground turmeric
1 bay leaf
1 package (10 ounces) frozen green peas, thawed
   and drained
   Pimiento strips
   Pitted ripe olives

Place chicken, skin sides up, in ungreased rectangular baking dish, 13 × 9 × 2 inches. Sprinkle with salt, paprika and pepper. Bake uncovered in 350° oven 30 minutes.

Heat broth to boiling. Remove chicken and drain fat from dish. Mix broth, rice, onion, garlic salt, oregano, turmeric, bay leaf and peas in baking dish. Top with chicken. Cover with aluminum foil and bake until rice and thickest pieces of chicken are done and liquid is absorbed, about 30 minutes. Remove bay leaf. Top with pimiento strips and olives. *6 servings.*

Brunswick Stew

Brunswick Stew

Georgia, North Carolina and Virginia all claim to be the birthplace of Brunswick Stew. We can say, for sure, that it is a southern specialty and a long-time favorite for church cookouts, political rallies, family reunions and other outdoor gatherings. Because no two recipes are ever alike, this country stew varies from place to place and season to season. Originally made with wild game such as squirrel, raccoon or opossum, most Brunswick Stew recipes in these tamer times call for chicken.

3- to 3½- pound broiler-fryer chicken, cut up
2 cups water
1½ teaspoons salt
¼ teaspoon pepper
   Dash of ground red pepper
2 cans (16 ounces each) whole tomatoes, undrained
1 can (17 ounces) whole kernel corn, undrained
1 can (16 ounces) lima beans, undrained
1 medium potato, cut into cubes (about 1 cup)
1 medium onion, chopped (about ½ cup)
¼ pound lean salt pork, cut into 1-inch pieces
½ cup cold water
2 tablespoons all-purpose flour

Remove any excess fat from chicken. Heat chicken, giblets, neck, 2 cups water and the salt to boiling in 5-quart Dutch oven; reduce heat. Cover and simmer until thickest pieces of chicken are tender, about 40 minutes.

Skim fat from broth. Remove skin and bones from chicken if desired; return chicken to broth. Stir in pepper, red pepper, tomatoes, corn, beans, potato, onion and pork. Heat to boiling; reduce heat. Simmer covered about 45 minutes. Shake ½ cup water and the flour in tightly covered container. Stir into stew. Heat to boiling, stirring constantly. Boil and stir 1 minute. *8 servings.*

Country Captain

Was this dish brought to the port of Savannah by the captain of a spice ship, as Georgians claim, or was it the invention of a local cook desperately tired of fried chicken? Whichever version they believed, cooks knew the exotic spices, blended to make curry powder today, would make a memorable dish when combined with plentiful regional foods. Among the Americans who enjoyed Country Captain was Franklin D. Roosevelt, who made sure it was often on the menu at the Summer White House in Warm Springs, Georgia.

½ cup all-purpose flour
1 teaspoon salt
¼ teaspoon pepper
2½- to 3-pound broiler-fryer chicken, cut up
¼ cup vegetable oil
1½ teaspoons curry powder
½ teaspoon dried thyme leaves
¼ teaspoon salt
1 large onion, chopped (about 1 cup)
1 green pepper, chopped (about 1½ cups)
1 clove garlic, finely chopped
1 can (16 ounces) whole tomatoes, undrained
¼ cup currants or raisins
⅓ cup slivered almonds, toasted
3 cups hot cooked rice

Heat oven to 350°. Mix flour, 1 teaspoon salt and the pepper. Coat chicken with flour mixture. Heat oil in 10-inch skillet until hot. Cook chicken over medium heat until light brown, 15 to 20 minutes. Place chicken in ungreased 2½-quart casserole. Drain oil from skillet.

Add curry powder, thyme, ¼ teaspoon salt, the onion, green pepper, garlic and tomatoes to skillet. Heat to boiling, stirring frequently to loosen brown particles from skillet. Pour over chicken. Cover and bake until thickest pieces are done, about 40 minutes. Skim fat from liquid if necessary; add currants. Bake uncovered 5 minutes. Sprinkle with almonds. Serve with rice and, if desired, grated fresh coconut and chutney. *6 servings.*

Chicken a la King

*Thought to have originated in the dining room of a popular Brighton Beach hotel outside New York City during the last quarter of the nineteenth century, Chicken a la King became synonymous with ladies' luncheons in the 1920s. The name is either a corruption of the French term **a la reine**, meaning in the queen's style, or a credit to the hotel's proprietors whose name was King.*

---

1 small green pepper, chopped (about ½ cup)
1 can (4 ounces) mushroom stems and pieces, drained (reserve liquid)
½ cup margarine or butter
½ cup all-purpose flour
1 teaspoon salt
¼ teaspoon pepper
1½ cups milk
1¼ cups chicken broth
2 cups cut-up cooked chicken
1 jar (2 ounces) chopped pimientos, drained
   Hot cooked rice, toasted bread triangles or patty shells

Cook and stir green pepper and mushrooms in margarine in 3-quart saucepan over medium heat 5 minutes. Stir in flour, salt and pepper. Cook over low heat, stirring constantly, until bubbly; remove from heat. Stir in milk, broth and reserved mushroom liquid. Heat to boiling, stirring constantly. Boil and stir 1 minute. Stir in chicken and pimientos; heat until hot. Serve over rice. *6 servings.*

Country Captain

Macaroni and Cheese

*Macaroni and Cheese is one of those plain, substantial dishes Americans love without realizing it has been around since before the American Revolution. Do you remember puzzling over the words in "Yankee Doodle" that say he "stuck a feather in his hat and called it macaroni"? At the time, macaroni was so popular among the English that it became a slang expression for anything that was exceptionally good or elegant. Because "Yankee Doodle" was written by a British soldier to make fun of the ragtag Continental soldiers, calling the feather **macaroni** was his way of describing their attempts to be as "elegant" as the better-equipped British forces.*

---

1 to 1½ cups uncooked elbow macaroni (about 6 ounces)
¼ cup margarine or butter
½ teaspoon salt
¼ teaspoon pepper
1 small onion, chopped (about ¼ cup)
¼ cup all-purpose flour
1¾ cups milk
8 ounces process American or sharp American cheese loaf or process cheese spread loaf, cut into ½-inch cubes

Cook macaroni as directed on package; drain. Cook and stir margarine, salt, pepper and onion in 2-quart saucepan over medium heat until onion is slightly tender. Stir in flour. Cook over low heat, stirring constantly, until smooth and bubbly; remove from heat. Stir in milk. Heat to boiling, stirring constantly. Boil and stir 1 minute; remove from heat. Stir in cheese until melted. Mix macaroni and cheese sauce in ungreased 1½-quart casserole. Bake uncovered in 375° oven 30 minutes. *5 servings.*

Ham Macaroni and Cheese: Mix 1 cup cut-up fully cooked smoked ham into cheese sauce. *7 servings.*

Pepper Macaroni and Cheese: Mix ⅓ cup chopped green and/or red pepper or 1 can (4 ounces) green chilies, drained and chopped, into cheese sauce.

Cheese Enchiladas

Enchiladas are standard fare in parts of the country where Mexican and Spanish influences are strong. Monterey Jack, a mild creamy cheese that bears the name both of a California community and of David Jacks, who first made the cheese in 1892, is an integral part of much Mexican-American cuisine.

---

1 large onion, chopped (about 1 cup)
2 large cloves garlic, crushed
1 tablespoon chili powder
2 tablespoons vegetable oil
1 can (28 ounces) whole tomatoes, undrained
1 teaspoon ground cumin
1 teaspoon dried oregano leaves
½ teaspoon salt
⅛ teaspoon pepper
1½ cups shredded Cheddar cheese (6 ounces)
1½ cups shredded Monterey Jack cheese (6 ounces)
¼ cup vegetable oil
1 package (8 or 9 ounces) 6- or 7-inch diameter corn tortillas (12 tortillas)
1½ cups shredded lettuce
½ cup sliced radishes
¼ cup sliced ripe olives
Dairy sour cream

Cook and stir onion, garlic and chili powder in 2 tablespoons oil in Dutch oven until onion is tender, about 5 minutes. Stir in tomatoes, cumin, oregano, salt and pepper; break up tomatoes with fork. Heat to boiling; reduce heat. Simmer uncovered until thickened, about 30 minutes.

Mix cheeses. Heat ¼ cup oil in 8-inch skillet until hot. Dip each tortilla lightly into hot oil to soften; drain. Dip each tortilla into sauce to coat both sides. Spoon about 2 tablespoons cheese onto each tortilla; roll tortilla around cheese. Place tortillas, seam sides down, in ungreased rectangular baking dish, 13 × 9 × 2 inches. Pour remaining tomato sauce over top; sprinkle with remaining cheese.

Bake uncovered in 350° oven until enchiladas are hot, about 15 minutes. Top with remaining ingredients. *6 servings.*

Cheese Enchiladas, Salsa Casera (page 11)

Boston Baked Beans

To some folks, it's just not Saturday night without baked beans and brown bread. Beans baking slowly in a traditional earthenware bean pot keeps alive the custom of their Puritan forebears, who did no cooking once the sun set on Saturday, marking the beginning of the Sabbath. Enjoy this most celebrated New England dish as it would be served at one of the old-fashioned baked bean suppers held throughout the region. Accompany the beans with Boston Brown Bread (page 61), Coleslaw (page 47) and India relish.

```
  6 cups water
1½ pounds dried navy beans (about 3 cups)
  1 large onion, sliced
 ¼ pound thinly sliced salt pork (with rind)
 ¼ cup packed brown sugar
 ¾ cup molasses
  1 teaspoon salt
  1 teaspoon dry mustard
 ⅛ teaspoon pepper
```

Heat water and beans to boiling in Dutch oven. Boil 2 minutes; remove from heat. Cover and let stand 1 hour. If necessary, add enough water to beans to cover. Heat to boiling; reduce heat. Cover and simmer until tender, 1 to 1½ hours (do not boil or beans will burst).

Drain beans, reserving liquid. Layer beans, onion and salt pork in ungreased 4-quart bean pot, casserole or Dutch oven. Mix brown sugar, molasses, salt, mustard, pepper and bean liquid; pour over beans. Add enough water to almost cover beans. Cover and bake in 350° oven 3 hours, stirring occasionally. Uncover and bake until beans are of desired consistency, about 30 minutes longer. *8 servings.*

New England Boiled Dinner

The pungent flavor of corned beef comes from the preservation method of pickling, the only way colonial farmers could keep valuable slaughtered beef for a long time. New England housewives simmered corned beef, along with cabbage and potatoes (contributed by Irish immigrants), to make a meat-on-a-platter that was sometimes served more than once a week. Horseradish, mustard and a choice of colorful pickles often accompany this New England favorite.

```
2-pound well-trimmed corned beef brisket
    or round
1 small onion, cut into fourths
1 clove garlic, crushed
6 small onions
6 medium carrots
3 potatoes, cut into halves
3 turnips, cut into cubes
1 small head green cabbage, cut into 6 wedges
```

Pour enough cold water on corned beef in Dutch oven just to cover. Add 1 small onion, cut into fourths, and the garlic. Heat to boiling; reduce heat. Cover and simmer until beef is almost tender, about 1 hour 40 minutes. Skim fat from broth. Add 6 onions, the carrots, potatoes and turnips. Cover and simmer 20 minutes. Remove beef; keep warm. Add cabbage. Heat to boiling; reduce heat. Simmer uncovered until vegetables are tender, about 15 minutes. *6 servings.*

Yankee Pot Roast of Beef

Across the country, the variations on pot roast are as distinctive as local accents. Chances are you have your own idea of the way a pot roast should be. Our Yankee version, browned and simmered slowly with root vegetables stored from summer's harvest, is one of the finest.

1/4 cup all-purpose flour
 2 teaspoons salt
1/2 teaspoon pepper
    4- to 5-pound boneless beef shoulder pot roast
 1 tablespoon vegetable oil or shortening
1/2 cup water
 2 cups sliced celery
 3 medium potatoes, pared and cut into
    1/2-inch cubes
 2 cups diced carrots
 2 cups 1/2-inch cubes rutabaga or yellow turnips
 1 cup chopped onion

Mix flour, salt and pepper; rub over beef roast. Heat oil in 12-inch skillet or Dutch oven until hot; brown beef on all sides. Drain fat from skillet; add water. Heat to boiling; reduce heat. Cover tightly and simmer on top of range or in 325° oven 2 hours.

Arrange vegetables around beef. Add 1/4 cup water if necessary. Cover and simmer, stirring vegetables occasionally, until beef and vegetables are tender, about 45 minutes. Remove beef and vegetables from skillet. Skim fat from broth; serve broth with beef. *12 servings.*

Chicken-fried Steak

Where large cattle herds range on the grasslands of the West and Southwest you'll find ranchers' families sitting down to meals of sustaining Chicken-fried Steak. Old-timers expect that the steak not be under-cooked, and they would be surprised if there were not a heaping bowl of mashed potatoes and plenty of Milk Gravy served with it.

---

1 1/2 pounds beef boneless round steak, about
       1/2 inch thick
   1 tablespoon water
   1 egg
   1 cup soda cracker crumbs (about 28 squares)
 1/4 teaspoon pepper
 1/4 cup vegetable oil
     Milk Gravy (below)

Cut beef steak into 6 serving pieces. Pound each piece until 1/4 inch thick to tenderize. Beat water and egg; reserve. Mix cracker crumbs and pepper. Dip beef into egg mixture, then coat with cracker crumbs. Heat oil in 12-inch skillet over medium-high heat until hot. Cook beef in oil, turning once, until brown, 6 to 7 minutes. Remove beef; keep warm. Prepare Milk Gravy; serve with chicken-fried steak. *6 servings.*

Milk Gravy

1/4 cup all-purpose flour
1/2 teaspoon salt
 2 cups milk

Measure drippings; add enough vegetable oil to drippings, if necessary, to measure 1/4 cup. Return drippings to skillet. Stir in flour and salt. Cook over low heat, stirring constantly to loosen brown particles from skillet, until smooth and bubbly; remove from heat. Slowly pour milk into skillet, stirring constantly. Heat to boiling over low heat, stirring constantly. Boil and stir 1 minute.

Venison Stew

Venison Stew

Venison was a staple in early North American cooking. In some parts of the country today, it is not uncommon to find a stockpile of game in home freezers just waiting to be turned into succulent, robust stews such as this one.

---

8 slices bacon, cut into ½-inch pieces
2 pounds boneless venison, cut into 1-inch cubes
4 cups water
2 cups dry red wine
1 teaspoon salt
½ teaspoon dried thyme leaves
½ teaspoon dried marjoram leaves
½ teaspoon pepper
8 ounces tiny pearl onions (about 2 cups)
4 medium carrots, cut into 1-inch pieces
2 large potatoes, cut into 1-inch pieces
1 cup cold water
⅓ cup all-purpose flour
1 teaspoon browning sauce, if desired
¼ cup snipped parsley

Cook bacon in 4-quart Dutch oven, stirring occasionally, until crisp. Remove bacon with slotted spoon; reserve. Cook and stir venison in bacon fat until brown, about 7 minutes. Add 2 cups water, the wine, salt, thyme, marjoram and pepper. Heat to boiling; reduce heat. Cover and simmer until venison is almost tender, about 2 hours.

Stir in onions, carrots and potato. Heat to boiling; reduce heat. Cover and simmer until vegetables are tender, about 30 minutes. Shake ½ cup cold water and the flour in tightly covered container; gradually stir into stew. Stir in browning sauce. Heat to boiling, stirring constantly. Boil and stir 1 minute. Sprinkle with bacon and parsley. *8 servings.*

Beef Stew: Substitute beef for the venison.

Texas Chili

Texas Chili

Although most people assume chili came across the border from Mexico, it is really a product of our own Southwest, where it has been avidly discussed and devoured for over a hundred years. Today, there is even a world-famous chili cook-off in Texas, the state where everyone knows what you mean when you order **a bowl of red**. Venison chili is a Lone Star specialty, but no self-respecting Texan would use ground beef or add beans to chili. If you're not a purist, Chili with Beans certainly is a delicious way to stretch out a few more servings!

3 pounds beef boneless round steak, cut into ½-inch cubes
3 tablespoons vegetable oil
½ cup snipped parsley
4 cups water
1 tablespoon paprika
1 tablespoon dried oregano leaves
2 teaspoons ground cumin
1½ teaspoons salt
1 to 2 teaspoons crushed red pepper
¾ teaspoon ground coriander
1 large bay leaf
3 large cloves garlic, crushed
1 large onion, chopped (about 1 cup)
1 can (8 ounces) tomato sauce
1 cup shredded Cheddar or Monterey Jack cheese (4 ounces)
1 cup dairy sour cream
1 medium avocado, chopped

Cook and stir half of the beef at a time in oil in Dutch oven over medium heat until light brown. Stir in parsley, water, seasonings, garlic, onion and tomato sauce. Heat to boiling; reduce heat. Cover and simmer 1 hour, stirring occasionally.

Uncover and simmer, stirring occasionally, until mixture thickens, about 1½ hours longer. Remove bay leaf. Serve with cheese, sour cream and avocado. *5 servings.*

Chili with Beans: Omit oil. Substitute ground beef for the beef steak; drain. After removing bay leaf, stir in 3 cans (15½ ounces each) pinto beans, undrained; heat to boiling. *8 servings.*

Venison Chili: Substitute venison for the beef.

Meat Loaf

Hearty, satisfying meat loaves are among the most popular ways Americans serve ground beef.

1½ pounds ground beef
1 cup milk
1 tablespoon Worcestershire sauce
1 teaspoon salt
½ teaspoon dry mustard
¼ teaspoon pepper
¼ teaspoon rubbed sage
⅛ teaspoon garlic powder
1 small onion, chopped (about ¼ cup)
3 slices bread, torn into small pieces*
1 egg
½ cup catsup, chili sauce or barbecue sauce

Mix all ingredients except catsup. Spread in ungreased loaf pan, 8½ × 4½ × 2½ or 9 × 5 × 3 inches, or shape into loaf in ungreased rectangular pan, 13 × 9 × 2 inches. Spoon catsup over top. Bake uncovered in 350° oven until done, 1 to 1¼ hours. Remove from pan. *6 servings.*

½ cup dry bread crumbs or ¾ cup quick-cooking oats can be substituted for the bread.

Individual Meat Loaves: Shape meat mixture into 6 small loaves; place in ungreased rectangular pan, 13 × 9 × 2 inches. Bake as directed except — decrease bake time to 45 minutes.

Spanish Meat Loaf: Omit sage. Substitute ⅓ cup tomato sauce and ⅔ cup milk for the milk. Mix in 8 large pimiento-stuffed olives, sliced. Substitute ⅔ cup tomato sauce for the catsup.

Salisbury Steak

These ground beef patties are named for Dr. J. H. Salisbury, a turn-of-the-century advocate who claimed that eating beef three times a day would lead to good health.

1 pound ground beef
⅓ cup dry bread crumbs
½ teaspoon salt
¼ teaspoon pepper
1 egg
1 large onion, sliced and separated into rings
1 can (10½ ounces) condensed beef broth
1 can (4 ounces) mushroom stems and pieces, drained
2 tablespoons cold water
2 teaspoons cornstarch

Mix ground beef, bread crumbs, salt, pepper and egg; shape into 4 oval patties, each about ¾ inch thick. Cook patties in 10-inch skillet over medium heat, turning occasionally, until brown, about 10 minutes; drain. Add onion, broth and mushrooms. Heat to boiling; reduce heat. Cover and simmer until beef is done, about 10 minutes.

Remove patties; keep warm. Heat onion mixture to boiling. Mix water and cornstarch; stir into onion mixture. Boil and stir 1 minute. Serve over patties. *4 servings.*

Fiesta Tamale Pie

*Tamales are made by steaming tamale dough made from **masa** (corn) and a filling of meat or beans in cornhusk wrappers. Tamale pie provides tamale flavors without the fuss, making this easily prepared main dish popular among Anglos throughout the Southwest.*

---

  1 pound ground beef
¼ pound bulk pork sausage
  1 small onion, chopped
  1 clove garlic, finely chopped
1½ teaspoons salt
1½ to 3 teaspoons chili powder
  1 can (16 ounces) whole tomatoes, undrained
  1 can (16 ounces) whole kernel corn, drained
20 to 24 pitted ripe olives
  1 cup cornmeal
  1 cup milk
  2 eggs, well beaten
  1 cup shredded Cheddar cheese (4 ounces)

Heat oven to 350°. Cook and stir ground beef, sausage, onion and garlic until meat is brown; drain. Stir in salt, chili powder, tomatoes, corn and olives. Heat to boiling. Pour into un-greased square baking dish, 8 × 8 × 2 inches, rectangular baking dish, 12 × 7½ × 2 inches, or 2-quart round casserole. Mix cornmeal, milk and eggs; pour over meat mixture. Sprinkle with cheese. Bake uncovered until golden brown, 40 to 50 minutes. *6 to 8 servings.*

Picadillo with Mexican Rice

Cooks in every region of Mexico prepare this special-ty, each one adding embellishments until no recipes are alike. Easy preparation and a delightful blend of flavors make Picadillo with Mexican Rice a favor-ite buffet dish wherever good Mexican food is enjoyed.

  Mexican Rice (below)
  1 medium onion, chopped (about ½ cup)
  2 tablespoons vegetable oil
  1 can (16 ounces) stewed tomatoes
  3 cups shredded cooked beef
¾ cup chopped green olives
½ cup raisins
  1 tablespoon capers
  1 teaspoon dried oregano leaves
  2 cloves garlic, finely chopped

Prepare Mexican Rice. Cook and stir onion in oil in 10-inch skillet until tender. Add toma-toes; cover and simmer 5 minutes. Stir in beef, olives, raisins, capers, oregano and garlic. Cover and simmer 15 minutes. Serve with Mex-ican Rice. *6 servings.*

Mexican Rice

  1 clove garlic, cut into halves
  2 tablespoons vegetable oil
  1 cup uncooked long grain white rice
  2 cups chicken broth
¼ cup Salsa Casera (page 11) or bottled salsa or picante sauce

Cook and stir garlic in oil in 2-quart saucepan over medium heat until brown; remove garlic. Cook and stir rice in oil until golden, about 5 minutes. Stir in broth and Salsa Casera. Heat to boiling, stirring occasionally; reduce heat. Cover and simmer 20 minutes. (Do not lift cover or stir.)

Lamb Barbecue

Grilled lamb is one of the unadorned preparations for lamb that Americans enjoy. Some of the most delicious lamb dishes in the American repertoire come from the immigrant sheepherders from the Basque provinces of the Pyrenees who settled in our western states nearly one hundred years ago.

   4- to 5-pound leg of lamb, boned
2 small cloves garlic, slivered
⅓ cup packed brown sugar
½ cup red wine vinegar
⅓ cup vegetable oil
2 tablespoons dried tarragon leaves
1 teaspoon salt
2 green onions (with tops), cut into 2-inch slices
1 can (8 ounces) tomato sauce

Trim excess fat from lamb; if necessary, cut lamb to lie flat. Cut 4 or 5 slits in lamb with tip of sharp knife; insert garlic slivers in slits. Mix remaining ingredients except tomato sauce; pour over lamb. Cover and refrigerate at least 8 hours, turning lamb 2 or 3 times.

Remove lamb; stir tomato sauce into marinade. Cover and grill lamb 5 to 6 inches from medium coals, turning every 10 minutes, until done (175°), 50 to 60 minutes; brush 2 or 3 times with marinade during last 10 minutes of grilling. Remove garlic slivers. *14 servings.*

Glazed Baked Ham

Hams have been country favorites for years because they could be cured and smoked to preserve them. The ham in this recipe can be purchased with the bone-in or boneless and has been completely cooked during processing. Only heating is needed before finishing with a sweet and spicy orange glaze. America is also famous for what are called "country hams" of which those from Smithfield, Virginia are most famous. Country hams are cured slowly in dry salt not in a salt brine, then smoked and aged to acquire their distinctive flavor. Country hams need extensive soaking and simmering before they can be baked.

¼ cup packed brown sugar
¼ teaspoon ground cloves
¼ teaspoon ground cinnamon
1 can (6 ounces) frozen orange juice concentrate (thawed)
   5- to 7-pound fully cooked smoked ham
   Whole cloves, if desired
   Cranberry Sauce (below)

Mix brown sugar, cloves, cinnamon and orange juice concentrate. Place ham, fat side up, on rack in shallow roasting pan. Insert meat thermometer so tip is in thickest part of ham and does not touch bone or rest in fat. Spoon or spread half of the juice mixture onto ham. Bake uncovered in 325° oven until heated through (140°), 1½ to 2 hours.

About 30 minutes before ham is done, remove from oven; pour drippings from pan. Cut fat surface of ham in uniform diamond pattern ¼ inch deep. Insert whole clove in each diamond. Spoon or spread remaining juice mixture on ham; continue baking 30 minutes. Garnish with orange slices if desired. Serve with Cranberry Sauce. *10 to 12 servings.*

Cranberry Sauce

1 can (16 ounces) whole berry cranberry sauce
1 teaspoon grated orange peel
½ teaspoon ground ginger
¼ teaspoon ground allspice

Heat all ingredients, stirring occasionally, until hot. Serve warm.

Fruit-stuffed Pork Roast

Pork roasts are popular company fare in the Midwest where many Swedish and Danish immigrants found homes. For them, pork roasted with a stuffing of dried fruit was a tradition to share with new neigh-bors. Our recipe takes these flavors of the old country and adds them to the popular boned pork loins found in today's markets.

½ teaspoon ground cinnamon
¼ teaspoon ground cloves
15 dried apricot halves (about 3 ounces)
9 pitted prunes (about 3 ounces)
   4-pound pork boneless top loin roast (double)
¾ teaspoon salt
¼ teaspoon pepper
1¼ cups apple cider
1 tablespoon cornstarch
1 tablespoon cold water

Sprinkle cinnamon and cloves over apricots and prunes; toss to coat. Stuff fruit lengthwise between the 2 pieces of pork roast in ribbon about 2 inches wide (work from both ends of roast). Sprinkle with salt and pepper.

Place pork, fat side up, on rack in shallow roasting pan. Insert meat thermometer so tip is in center of thickest part of pork and does not rest in fat or fruit mixture. Roast uncovered in 325° oven until thermometer registers 170°, about 2½ hours. After 1½ hours, brush occasionally with ¼ cup of the cider.

Remove pork and rack from pan; keep pork warm. Pour remaining cider into roasting pan; stir to loosen brown particles. Mix cornstarch and water; stir into cider mixture. Heat to boiling, stirring constantly. Boil and stir 1 minute. Serve with pork. *12 servings.*

Fruit-stuffed Pork Roast

Stuffed Pork Chops

Double thick pork chops with sage-flavored stuffing are a Sunday dinner specialty in the farmlands of the Midwest.

⅓ cup chopped celery (with leaves)
3 tablespoons finely chopped onion
¼ cup margarine or butter
2¼ cups soft bread cubes (about 4 slices bread)
½ teaspoon salt
¼ teaspoon rubbed sage
¼ teaspoon dried thyme leaves
⅛ teaspoon pepper
4 pork loin chops, about 1 inch thick (with pockets cut into chops)
2 tablespoons vegetable oil
¼ cup apple juice or water

Cook and stir celery and onion in margarine in 2-quart saucepan over medium heat, stirring frequently, until celery is tender; remove from heat. Stir in bread, salt, sage, thyme and pepper.

Stuff each pork chop pocket with about ⅓ cup of the bread mixture. Fasten by inserting 2 wooden picks in X shape through edges of pork. Cook in oil in 10-inch skillet over medium heat until brown on both sides, about 15 minutes; drain. Add apple juice; reduce heat. Cover and simmer until pork chops are done, about 1 hour. Remove wooden picks. *4 servings.*

Barbecued Spareribs

Like many culinary terms, barbecue derives its name from a description of a method of cooking. In Spanish, **barbacoa** *means an elevated framework of sticks, one of the oldest cooking methods and the one most suited to the slow cooking of whole game. By now, the enormous barbecues of the Southwest have been adapted to almost every backyard in America. And Americans barbecue spareribs more than almost any other meat.*

4½-pound rack fresh pork loin back ribs
3 cups water
Spicy Barbecue Sauce (below)

Place pork ribs in Dutch oven; add water. Heat to boiling; reduce heat. Cover and simmer 5 minutes; drain.

Cover and grill pork 5 to 6 inches from medium coals, brushing with Spicy Barbecue Sauce every 3 minutes, until done and meat begins to pull away from bones (170°), 15 to 20 minutes. Serve with remaining sauce. *6 servings.*

Spicy Barbecue Sauce

⅓ cup margarine or butter
2 tablespoons vinegar
2 tablespoons water
1 teaspoon sugar
½ teaspoon garlic powder
½ teaspoon onion powder
½ teaspoon pepper
Dash of ground red pepper

Heat all ingredients, stirring frequently, until margarine is melted.

Oven Barbecued Spareribs: Do not boil ribs; cut into serving pieces and place, meaty sides up, on rack in shallow roasting pan. Roast uncovered in 325° oven 1½ hours. Brush with sauce. Roast, turning and brushing frequently with sauce, until done, about 45 minutes longer.

Sweet-and-Sour Pork

Few Chinese dishes have endeared themselves to Americans more than Sweet-and-Sour Pork.

2 pounds pork boneless top loin
   Vegetable oil
½ cup all-purpose flour
¼ cup cornstarch
½ cup cold water
1 teaspoon salt
1 egg
1 can (20 ounces) pineapple chunks in syrup,
   drained (reserve syrup)
½ cup packed brown sugar
½ cup vinegar
1 teaspoon salt
2 teaspoons soy sauce
2 carrots, cut diagonally into thin slices
1 clove garlic, finely chopped
2 tablespoons cornstarch
2 tablespoons cold water
1 green pepper, cut into ¾-inch pieces
   Hot cooked rice

Trim excess fat from pork; cut pork into ¾-inch pieces. Heat oil (1 inch) in deep fryer or Dutch oven to 360°. Beat flour, ¼ cup cornstarch, ½ cup cold water, 1 teaspoon salt and the egg in 3-quart bowl with hand beater until smooth. Stir pork into batter until well coated. Add pork pieces, one at a time, to oil. Fry about 20 pieces at a time, turning 2 or 3 times, until golden brown, about 5 minutes; drain and keep warm.

Add enough water to reserved pineapple syrup to measure 1 cup. Heat syrup mixture, brown sugar, vinegar, 1 teaspoon salt, the soy sauce, carrots and garlic to boiling in Dutch oven; reduce heat. Cover and simmer until carrots are crisp-tender, about 6 minutes. Mix 2 tablespoons cornstarch and 2 tablespoons cold water; stir into sauce. Add pork, pineapple and green pepper. Heat to boiling, stirring constantly. Boil and stir 1 minute. Serve with rice. *8 servings.*

Sweet-and-Sour Pork

Pork Chow Mein

*Feeding the crews of Chinese workers who were brought to America to build the great transcontinental railroads was not easy. The railroad cooks had only a vague notion of the **chow** that would satisfy these willing workers from the Orient. Adapting ingredients that were readily available and could be easily cooked, the cooks created two flavorful (and completely American) dishes: chop suey and chow mein.*

---

1 pound pork blade or arm steak, cut into thin strips
1 tablespoon vegetable oil
2 cups beef broth
2 tablespoons soy sauce
2 medium stalks celery, sliced (about 1 cup)
1 medium onion, chopped (about ½ cup)
1 can (4 ounces) mushroom stems and pieces, drained (reserve ¼ cup liquid)
3 tablespoons cornstarch
1 can (16 ounces) Chinese vegetables, drained
1 tablespoon brown gravy sauce (molasses type)
3 cups chow mein noodles

Cook and stir pork in oil in 10-inch skillet over medium heat until brown. Stir in broth, soy sauce, celery and onion. Heat to boiling; reduce heat. Cover and simmer 30 minutes.

Shake reserved mushroom liquid and the cornstarch in tightly covered container; gradually stir into pork mixture. Add mushrooms, Chinese vegetables and gravy sauce. Heat to boiling, stirring constantly. Boil and stir 1 minute. Serve over noodles. *5 servings.*

Sausage and Bean Casserole

*Lima beans, pea beans, kidney beans — Americans grow an abundance of beans. No wonder hearty casseroles (Americanized versions of the **cassoulets** of France) like this one have been such great standbys for family meals.*

---

1 package (10 ounces) frozen lima beans
1 can (21 ounces) baked beans
1 can (15½ ounces) kidney beans, drained
½ pound Italian or pork link sausages
½ cup catsup
1 tablespoon packed brown sugar
½ teaspoon salt
½ teaspoon dry mustard
⅛ teaspoon pepper
1 small onion, chopped (about ¼ cup)

Cook lima beans as directed on package; drain. Mix lima beans, baked beans and kidney beans in ungreased 2-quart casserole. Heat sausages and small amount of water to boiling; reduce heat. Cover and simmer 5 minutes; drain. Cook sausages until brown on all sides (do not prick sausages). Cut sausages into bite-size pieces; stir into beans. Mix remaining ingredients; stir into bean mixture. Bake uncovered in 400° oven until hot and bubbly, 40 to 50 minutes. *6 servings.*

Ham and Bean Casserole: Substitute ¾ cup cut-up fully cooked smoked ham for the cooked sausages.

Homespun Sausage Pie

Homespun Sausage Pie

The inspiration for this hearty main-dish pie comes from the resourceful immigrants who came from Central Europe. When making the pie with the lattice-and-braid crust in the photograph, allow enough pastry for a two-crust pie.

1½ pounds bulk pork sausage
½ cup chopped onion
1 tablespoon sugar
1½ teaspoons salt
1 medium head green cabbage (1¾ pounds), cut into large chunks and cored
1 can (16 ounces) whole tomatoes, undrained
Pastry for 9-inch one-crust pie
2 tablespoons all-purpose flour
¼ cup cold water

Cook and stir sausage and onion in Dutch oven until sausage is done; drain. Stir in sugar, salt, cabbage and tomatoes. Heat to boiling; reduce heat. Cover and simmer 10 minutes.

Heat oven to 400°. Prepare pastry; shape into flattened round on lightly floured cloth-covered board. Roll to fit top of 2-quart casserole. Fold into fourths; cut slits so steam can escape.

Mix flour and water; stir into hot sausage mixture. Pour into ungreased casserole. Place pastry over top and unfold; seal pastry to edge of casserole. Bake until crust is brown, 25 to 30 minutes. *6 servings.*

Accompaniments

Coleslaw

*Cabbage is sliced, chopped, shredded and even grated into bowls and bowls of the salad Americans call coleslaw. The name comes from the Anglicized Dutch words **cool** for cabbage and **sla** for salad. There are as many different ways to prepare coleslaw as there are regions in this country. Here are three flavor variations that have been favorites through the years.*

---

1 cup dairy sour cream or plain yogurt
½ cup mayonnaise or salad dressing
2 teaspoons sugar
1 teaspoon dry mustard
1 teaspoon seasoned salt
¼ teaspoon pepper
1 medium head cabbage, finely shredded or chopped (about 8 cups)
1 medium onion, chopped (about ½ cup)

Mix sour cream, mayonnaise, sugar, mustard, seasoned salt and pepper; toss with cabbage and onion. Sprinkle with paprika or dried dill weed if desired. *8 servings.*

Apple-Cheese Coleslaw: Omit onion; toss 1 pared or unpared eating apple, chopped, and ¼ cup crumbled blue cheese with the cabbage.

Pineapple-Marshmallow Coleslaw: Omit onion; toss 1 can (8 ounces) crushed pineapple in juice, drained, and 1 cup miniature marshmallows with the cabbage.

Coleslaw, Hush Puppies (page 59), Southern-fried Catfish (page 24)

Peas and Cheese Salad

Salads from America's heartland reflect the region's tradition of serving food for hearty appetites. You'll find Peas and Cheese Salad on the bountiful buffet tables of neighborhood potluck gatherings, still the favorite way to entertain in the Midwest.

⅓ to ½ cup mayonnaise or salad dressing
½ teaspoon salt
½ teaspoon prepared mustard
¼ teaspoon sugar
⅛ teaspoon pepper
1 package (10 ounces) frozen green peas, thawed and drained
1 cup diced mild Cheddar or colby cheese
1 medium stalk celery, thinly sliced (about ⅓ cup)
3 sweet pickles, chopped (about ¼ cup)
2 tablespoons finely chopped onion
2 hard-cooked eggs, chopped

Mix mayonnaise, salt, mustard, sugar and pepper in 2½-quart bowl. Add peas, cheese, celery, pickles and onion; toss. Stir in eggs. Cover and refrigerate until chilled, at least 1 hour. Serve on lettuce leaves if desired. Immediately refrigerate any remaining salad. *6 servings.*

Kidney Bean and Cheese Salad: Substitute 1 can (15 ounces) kidney beans, rinsed and drained, for the peas.

Hot German Potato Salad

Another of those famous recipes for which the Pennsylvania Dutch receive credit.

1½ pounds potatoes (about 4 medium)
 3 slices bacon
 1 medium onion, chopped (about ½ cup)
 1 tablespoon all-purpose flour
 1 tablespoon sugar
 1 teaspoon salt
¼ teaspoon celery seed
   Dash of pepper
½ cup water
¼ cup vinegar

Heat 1 inch salted water (½ teaspoon salt to 1 cup water) to boiling. Add potatoes. Cover and heat to boiling; reduce heat. Cook until tender, 30 to 35 minutes; drain.

Cook bacon in 8-inch skillet until crisp; remove bacon and drain. Cook and stir onion in bacon fat until tender. Stir in flour, sugar, salt, celery seed and pepper. Cook over low heat, stirring constantly, until bubbly; remove from heat. Stir in water and vinegar. Heat to boiling, stirring constantly. Boil and stir 1 minute; remove from heat. Crumble bacon into hot mixture, then slice in warm potatoes. Cook, stirring gently to coat potato slices, until hot and bubbly. *5 servings.*

Country Potato Salad

Some of the best potato salads — coleslaws, too — of days gone by were tossed with homemade cooked salad dressings. This one is like the colorful country classics of the Great Plains. Using springtime new potatoes and marinating them while warm, French style, are keys to the tastiest potato salads.

---

 2 pounds potatoes (about 6 medium)
¼ cup Italian dressing
   Cooked Salad Dressing (below) or 1 cup
     mayonnaise or salad dressing
 1 cup sliced celery
 1 cup chopped cucumber
¾ cup chopped onion
½ cup thinly sliced radishes
 4 hard-cooked eggs, chopped

Heat 1 inch salted water (½ teaspoon salt to 1 cup water) to boiling. Add potatoes. Cover and heat to boiling; reduce heat. Cook until tender, 30 to 35 minutes. Drain and cool slightly; cut into cubes. Toss warm potatoes with Italian dressing in 4-quart glass or plastic bowl. Cover and refrigerate at least 4 hours. Prepare Cooked Salad Dressing.

Add remaining ingredients to potatoes. Pour Cooked Salad Dressing over top; toss. Refrigerate until chilled. Immediately refrigerate any remaining salad. *10 servings.*

Cooked Salad Dressing

 2 tablespoons all-purpose flour
 1 tablespoon sugar
 1 teaspoon dry mustard
¾ teaspoon salt
¼ teaspoon pepper
 1 egg yolk, slightly beaten
¾ cup milk
 2 tablespoons vinegar
 1 tablespoon margarine or butter

Mix flour, sugar, mustard, salt and pepper in 1-quart saucepan. Mix egg yolk and milk; slowly stir into flour mixture. Cook over medium heat, stirring constantly, until mixture thickens and boils. Boil and stir 1 minute; remove from heat. Stir in vinegar and margarine. Place plastic wrap directly on surface; refrigerate until cool, at least 1 hour.

Wilted Spinach Salad

Women who made the frontier their home relied on edible wild greens to contribute fresh vegetables to meals. Sweet-sour flavors were a good match for the greens' pungent flavors. Spinach, usually the first spring garden crop, was welcomed to winter-weary households using this same sweet-sour preparation.

---

1 medium onion, chopped (about ½ cup)
1 slice bacon, cut up
1 clove garlic, finely chopped
2 tablespoons margarine or butter
2 tablespoons olive or vegetable oil
½ teaspoon salt
¼ teaspoon pepper
¼ teaspoon ground nutmeg
1 pound spinach
  Juice of ½ lemon (about 2 tablespoons)

Cook and stir onion, bacon and garlic in margarine and oil in Dutch oven over medium heat until bacon is crisp; reduce heat. Stir in salt, pepper and nutmeg. Add spinach; toss just until spinach is wilted. Drizzle with lemon juice. *6 servings.*

Creamy Cucumber Salad

Americans have long enjoyed thinly sliced cucumbers in creamy dressings. It is little wonder since cucumbers appear in the ethnic cuisine of immigrants from Scandinavia to the Mediterranean to the Orient.

½ cup mayonnaise, salad dressing or plain yogurt
½ teaspoon salt
¼ teaspoon dried dill weed
⅛ teaspoon pepper
2 medium cucumbers, thinly sliced
1 small onion, thinly sliced and separated
  into rings

Mix all ingredients. Cover and refrigerate at least 4 hours. *7 servings.*

Stuffed Tomato Salads

Ruby red tomatoes make beautiful containers for all-American corn and peppers. Home gardeners in America grow tomatoes more often than any other vegetable.

---

8 large tomatoes, cut into halves
¼ cup sliced green onions (with tops)
⅓ cup vegetable oil
2 tablespoons snipped parsley
2 tablespoons vinegar
1 teaspoon dried basil leaves
½ teaspoon salt
1 can (16 ounces) whole kernel corn, drained
1 small green pepper, chopped (about ½ cup)

Remove pulp from each tomato half, leaving a ¼-inch wall; chop enough pulp to measure ½ cup. Mix pulp and remaining ingredients. Fill tomatoes with corn mixture. Cover and refrigerate at least 3 hours. *8 servings.*

Twenty-four Hour Salad

The ready availability of canned fruits and fresh fruit in season made salads like this a popular choice for buffets and potluck suppers.

Whipped Cream Dressing (below)
1 can (16½ ounces) pitted light or dark sweet cherries, drained
2 cans (13¼ ounces each) pineapple chunks in syrup, drained (reserve 2 tablespoons syrup)
3 oranges, pared, sectioned and cut up, or 2 cans (11 ounces each) mandarin orange segments, drained
1 cup miniature marshmallows

Prepare Whipped Cream Dressing; toss with remaining ingredients. Cover and refrigerate at least 12 hours but no longer than 24 hours. Immediately refrigerate any remaining salad. *8 servings.*

Whipped Cream Dressing

2 tablespoons sugar
2 tablespoons vinegar or lemon juice
2 tablespoons reserved pineapple syrup
1 tablespoon margarine or butter
  Dash of salt
2 eggs, beaten
¾ cup chilled whipping cream

Heat all ingredients except whipping cream just to boiling, stirring constantly; cool. Beat whipping cream in chilled 1½-quart bowl until stiff; fold in egg mixture.

West Coast Orange Salad

Having a year-round supply of fresh fruits and vegetables is the secret to the imaginative style of California cooking. A good example is this tossed salad mixed with honey-tinged dressing and the West's own oranges, walnuts and, what else, the avocado.

Orange-Walnut Dressing (below)
4 cups bite-size pieces salad greens
4 ounces mushrooms, sliced (about 1½ cups)
2 oranges, pared and sectioned

Prepare Orange-Walnut Dressing; toss with remaining ingredients. *6 servings.*

Orange-Walnut Dressing

½ cup coarsely chopped walnuts
¼ cup vegetable oil
¼ cup orange juice
2 teaspoons honey
1 teaspoon finely shredded orange peel
½ teaspoon celery salt
¼ teaspoon dry mustard

Shake all dressing ingredients in tightly covered container.

West Coast Avocado-Orange Salad: Add 1 avocado, cut into ¼-inch slices.

Waldorf Salad

Waldorf Salad

Two parts diced apples to one part celery, tossed in mayonnaise, served on crisp lettuce. *That was the original recipe for this classic salad; the nuts were added later. Named for a great New York hotel,* *this salad was served at a society supper prior to the hotel's grand opening. Today, Waldorf Salad and its many variations are remembered as some of the comfort foods one enjoyed eating in grandma's kitchen.*

2 medium eating apples, coarsely chopped
   (about 2 cups)
2 medium stalks celery, chopped (about 1 cup)
½ cup mayonnaise or salad dressing
⅓ cup coarsely chopped nuts

Toss all ingredients. Serve on salad greens if desired. *4 servings.*

Pear Waldorf Salad: Substitute 4 pears, coarsely chopped, for the apples.

Waldorf Salad Supreme: Decrease celery to 1 medium stalk and nuts to ¼ cup. Stir in 1 can (8¼ ounces) pineapple chunks in syrup, drained, ½ cup miniature marshmallows and ⅓ cup cut-up dates.

Waldorf Salad with Grapes: Decrease celery to 1 medium stalk. Stir in 1 cup grapes, cut into halves and seeded.

Cranberry Salad Mold

Early settlers learned to cook with cranberries from the Indians of the Cape Cod area. Cranberries are an essential addition to Thanksgiving feasts whether served as relish or molded salad. The gelatin-based salads gained in popularity only after the electric refrigerator became a fairly common household appliance in the 1930s.

¾ cup boiling water
1 package (3 ounces) raspberry-flavored gelatin
½ cup coarsely chopped nuts
⅓ cup chopped celery
1 can (16 ounces) whole berry cranberry sauce
1 can (8¼ ounces) crushed pineapple in syrup, undrained

Pour boiling water on gelatin in 2-quart bowl; stir until gelatin is dissolved. Stir in remaining ingredients. Pour into 5-cup mold. Refrigerate until firm; unmold. Garnish with salad greens if desired. *8 servings.*

Perfection Salad

The original Perfection Salad won a Pennsylvania woman a hundred-dollar sewing machine in a turn-of-the-century cooking contest. By the 1930s, electric refrigerators and sweetened flavored gelatins encouraged a new generation to create the hundreds of gelatin salad recipes prevalent in American cooking.

---

1 cup boiling water
1 package (3 ounces) lemon-flavored gelatin
1 cup cold water
2 tablespoons lemon juice or vinegar
1 teaspoon salt
1 cup finely chopped celery
1 cup finely shredded cabbage
⅓ cup chopped sweet pickles
2 tablespoons finely chopped pimientos

Pour boiling water on gelatin in 2-quart bowl; stir until gelatin is dissolved. Stir in water, lemon juice and salt. Refrigerate until slightly thickened but not set. Stir in remaining ingredients. Pour into 4-cup mold or 6 individual molds. Refrigerate until firm; unmold. *6 servings.*

Harvard Beets

How the name of an Ivy League university became attached to a New England recipe for beets seems to be lost in time. Some attribute the name to Harvard red, one of the school colors. That the almost identical Yale Beets came about because the Harvard version was often poorly prepared is probably a story only encouraged by someone with this traditional rival's sympathies. Whichever is chosen, these flavorful classics will brighten the most ordinary meals.

1 tablespoon cornstarch
1 tablespoon sugar
¾ teaspoon salt
    Dash of pepper
⅔ cup water
¼ cup vinegar
5 medium beets (about 1¼ pounds), cooked
    and sliced

Mix cornstarch, sugar, salt and pepper in 1½-quart saucepan. Gradually stir in water and vinegar. Cook, stirring constantly, until mixture thickens and boils. Boil and stir 1 minute. Stir in beets; heat through. *4 servings.*

Easy Harvard Beets: Substitute 1 can (16 ounces) sliced beets, drained (reserve liquid), for the fresh beets. Add enough water to reserved beet liquid to measure ⅔ cup. Substitute beet liquid mixture for the water.

Yale Beets: Substitute packed brown sugar for the sugar and ¾ cup orange juice for the water. Mix in 1 teaspoon grated orange peel with the sugar. Decrease vinegar to 1 tablespoon.

Fried Cabbage, Country Style

One of the characteristics of country-style cooking in the South is the touch of bacon or salt pork added to vegetables. A recipe similar to this one is also found among the Basque population of our western mountain states. Cabbage has a timeless appeal and is used in countless recipes across America. The use of red cabbage is most associated with the cooking brought to this country by German immigrants.

2 tablespoons bacon fat
1 medium head green cabbage (about 1¼
    pounds), shredded
2 tablespoons whipping cream
1½ teaspoons lemon juice or vinegar
    Salt and pepper

Heat bacon fat in 10-inch skillet. Add cabbage. Cook over low heat, stirring frequently, until light brown. Cover and cook, stirring occasionally, until crisp-tender, about 5 minutes. Stir in whipping cream and lemon juice; heat until cream is hot. Sprinkle with salt and pepper. *4 servings.*

Fried Red Cabbage: Substitute vegetable oil for the bacon fat and red cabbage for the green cabbage.

Cheesy Grits

*Corn kernels that are dried, soaked in wood-ash lye to remove the outer hulls, then washed to a snowy white are another of the indigenous American foods the Europeans learned to prepare from the Indians. Called hominy, from the Algonkian Indian word, **tackhummin,** meaning grind corn, it became known as the "potatoes of the South." When ground into smaller particles, hominy becomes another Southern favorite, grits. This deep South specialty, Cheesy Grits, is a traditional accompaniment to turkey, quail or other game birds.*

---

2 cups milk
2 cups water
1 teaspoon salt
¼ teaspoon pepper
1 cup hominy quick grits
1½ cups shredded Cheddar cheese (6 ounces)
¼ cup sliced green onions (with tops)
2 eggs, slightly beaten
1 tablespoon margarine or butter
¼ teaspoon paprika

Heat milk, water, salt and pepper to boiling in 2-quart saucepan. Gradually add grits, stirring constantly; reduce heat. Simmer uncovered, stirring frequently, until thick, about 5 minutes. Stir in cheese and onions. Stir 1 cup of the hot mixture into eggs; stir into remaining hot mixture in saucepan. Pour into greased 1½-quart casserole. Dot with margarine; sprinkle with paprika. Bake uncovered in 350° oven until set, 35 to 40 minutes. Let stand 10 minutes. Immediately refrigerate any remaining grits. *8 servings.*

Mexican Succotash

In the same manner that the Pilgrims learned to grow corn and beans from the Indians living near Plymouth, Spanish settlers were introduced to corn and squash by Indians of the Southwest. What the Pilgrims called succotash — hominy and cranberry beans in winter, fresh corn and lima beans in summer — is in other regions of America those hearty stewed vegetable medleys of which Mexican Succotash is an example. Corn has a natural affinity for tomatoes, squash, beans, okra and peppers and has always been central to these colorful side dishes.

---

3 medium zucchini
2 ears corn*
1 medium onion, chopped (about ½ cup)
¼ cup vegetable oil
1 can (28 ounces) Italian plum tomatoes
1 teaspoon salt
1 teaspoon dried oregano leaves
   Dash of pepper

Cut zucchini into ½-inch slices. Cut kernels from corn. Cook and stir onion in oil in 10-inch skillet over medium heat until tender. Add zucchini; cook and stir 1 minute. Stir in corn and remaining ingredients. Heat to boiling; reduce heat. Cover and simmer until zucchini is tender, about 15 minutes. *6 servings.*

*1 package (10 ounces) frozen corn can be substituted for the ears of corn.

French-fried Onions

French-fried Onions

Because they have a slightly sweet flavor, the large yellow onion varieties called either Spanish or Bermuda are the cook's choice for crispy onion rings. In earlier days, before French fries came to mean only potatoes, French-fried Onions were always the traditional accompaniment to a steak dinner.

Vegetable oil
¾ cup all-purpose flour
½ cup milk
½ teaspoon salt
1 egg
3 large Spanish or Bermuda onions, cut into
   ¼-inch slices and separated into rings

Heat oil (1 inch) in deep fryer or Dutch oven to 375°. Beat remaining ingredients except onion rings with hand beater until smooth. Dip each onion ring into batter, allowing excess to drip into bowl. Fry a few onion rings at a time in hot oil, turning once, until golden brown, about 2 minutes; drain. Keep warm in 300° oven while frying remaining onion rings. *4 servings.*

Farm-fried Potatoes

Potatoes were a mainstay of pioneer times. Old varieties such as Irish Cobbler, Katahdin and Red Bliss were grown because of their unique flavors or keeping qualities. One may find them today only in local markets or grown by gardeners with a flair for experimentation. Likewise, many recipes from yesteryear can lend a change of pace to mealtimes. These raw fried potatoes are a crisper cousin of hashed brown potatoes. The Russet Burbank potatoes that grow in abundance in Idaho are widely available and a good choice for this recipe.

---

2 tablespoons vegetable oil or shortening
2 pounds potatoes (about 6 medium), thinly sliced
   (about 4 cups)
1 large onion, thinly sliced, if desired
1½ teaspoons salt
   Pepper
2 tablespoons margarine or butter

Heat oil in 10-inch skillet until hot. Layer ⅓ each of the potatoes and onion in skillet; sprinkle with ½ teaspoon of the salt and dash of pepper. Repeat 2 times. Dot with margarine. Cover and cook over medium heat 20 minutes. Uncover and cook, turning once, until potatoes are brown. *4 servings.*

Candied Sweet Potatoes

*Sweet potatoes and yams, at least those currently grown in warmer regions of the United States, are **both** varieties of sweet potatoes. One, a deep orange color and moister when cooked, is marketed as the yam. Southern cooks prefer "yams" to what are sometimes called Jersey Sweets, the creamy yellow variety of sweet potatoes that are drier when cooked. Because either variety blends well with other flavors, America's cooks have come up with dozens of recipes, among them the favorite regional variations we've included.*

---

2 pounds sweet potatoes or yams (about
   6 medium)*
½ cup packed brown sugar
3 tablespoons margarine or butter
3 tablespoons water
½ teaspoon salt

Heat enough salted water to cover potatoes (½ teaspoon salt to 1 cup water) to boiling. Add potatoes. Cover and heat to boiling; reduce heat. Boil until tender, 30 to 35 minutes. Drain and cool slightly. Slip off skins. Cut potatoes into ½-inch slices.

Heat remaining ingredients in 8-inch skillet over medium heat, stirring constantly, until smooth and bubbly. Add potato slices; stir gently until glazed and hot. *4 to 6 servings.*

*1 can (23 ounces) sweet potatoes or yams, drained and cut into ½-inch slices can be substituted for sweet potatoes.

Brandy Sweet Potatoes: Substitute brandy for the water.

Orange Sweet Potatoes: Substitute orange juice for the water and add 1 tablespoon grated orange peel.

Pineapple Sweet Potatoes: Omit water; add 1 can (8¼ ounces) crushed pineapple in syrup, undrained.

Spicy Sweet Potatoes: Stir ½ teaspoon ground cinnamon or ¼ teaspoon ground allspice, cloves, mace or nutmeg into brown sugar mixture in skillet.

Blue Cornmeal Muffins

Corn is the most American of grains. Breads made from cornmeal are among our favorite regional specialties. In Arizona and New Mexico, the Hopi Indians cultivate six varieties of corn — white, yellow, red, blue, black and speckled — each used in a different manner. Blue cornmeal, available in specialty food stores and catalogs, is used in both Hopi and Navaho cooking for breads and tortillas.

1¼ cups blue or yellow cornmeal
 ¾ cup all-purpose flour
 ¼ cup shortening
 2 teaspoons baking powder
 1 teaspoon sugar
 1 teaspoon salt
 ½ teaspoon baking soda
1½ cups buttermilk
 2 eggs

Heat oven to 450°. Grease bottoms only of 14 medium muffin cups, 2½ × 1¼ inches, or line with paper baking cups. Mix all ingredients; beat vigorously 30 seconds. Fill muffin cups about ⅞ full. Bake until light golden brown, 20 to 25 minutes. Immediately remove from pan. *14 muffins.*

Honey-Nut Muffins

Muffins, although uniquely American, share both an English and German origin. A shaker for sugar called a **muffineer** *was a tool used by English cooks to sprinkle sugar on cakes. In the same tradition, this recipe suggests sprinkling the muffins with sugar before baking. In recent years, muffins have been transformed. The health food movement of the late 1970s changed their cakelike predecessors to the heartier, healthier muffins of today.*

---

 1 egg
¾ cup milk
½ cup chopped nuts
⅓ cup vegetable oil
¼ cup honey
 2 cups all-purpose or whole wheat flour
 3 teaspoons baking powder
½ teaspoon salt

Heat oven to 400°. Grease bottoms only of about 12 medium muffin cups, 2½ × 1¼ inches. Beat egg in 2½-quart bowl; stir in milk, nuts, oil and honey. Stir in remaining ingredients all at once just until flour is moistened (batter will be lumpy). Fill muffin cups about ¾ full; sprinkle with sugar if desired. Bake until golden brown, about 20 minutes. Immediately remove from pan. *About 12 muffins.*

Blueberry Muffins: Stir in 1 cup fresh or ¾ cup frozen (thawed and well drained) blueberries with the milk. Sprinkle tops with mixture of ¼ cup packed brown sugar and ½ teaspoon ground cinnamon before baking if desired.

Bran Muffins: Increase milk to 1½ cups. Pour milk over 1½ cups whole wheat bran cereal; let stand 2 minutes. Stir in with the oil.

Dixie Biscuits

Rich and tender on the outside, soft and fluffy on the inside is the hallmark of a true Southern-style biscuit. Many Southern cooks still serve biscuits fresh from the oven for breakfast, lunch and dinner, encouraging guests to "take two, and butter them while they're hot." Dixie Biscuits reflect the best of the Southern tradition — thinner biscuits with fork-pricked golden tops.

1¾ cups all-purpose flour or 2 cups cake flour
2½ teaspoons baking powder
¾ teaspoon salt*
⅓ cup shortening or firm margarine or butter
¾ cup milk

Heat oven to 425°. Mix flour, baking powder and salt. Cut in shortening until mixture resembles fine crumbs. Stir in almost all the milk. Stir in just enough additional milk to make a soft, puffy, easy-to-roll dough. (Too much milk makes dough sticky, not enough makes biscuits dry.)

Shape dough into ball on lightly floured cloth-covered surface. (If using all-purpose flour, knead about 10 times.) Pat into circle about ½ inch thick with floured hands. Fold into thirds; pat again into circle about ½ inch thick. Cut with floured 1¾-inch biscuit cutter.

Place on ungreased cookie sheet 1 inch apart for crusty sides, close together for soft sides. Prick each biscuit several times with fork. Brush with slightly beaten egg or evaporated milk if desired. Bake until golden brown, 12 to 15 minutes. Serve hot. *About 16 biscuits.*

*If using margarine or butter, decrease salt to ½ teaspoon.

Popovers

Popovers achieve their spectacular showiness using a batter that is similar to the one for pancakes. The inspiration for this popular hot bread was the English Yorkshire pudding.

2 eggs
1 cup all-purpose flour
1 cup milk
½ teaspoon salt

Heat oven to 450°. Generously grease six 6-ounce custard cups. Beat eggs slightly; beat in remaining ingredients just until smooth (do not overbeat). Fill custard cups about ½ full. Bake 20 minutes. Decrease oven temperature to 350°; bake 20 minutes longer. Immediately remove from cups; serve hot. *6 popovers.*

Fluffy Spoon Bread

Spoon bread is hardly corn bread at all except for its crusty outside. Rich with eggs and buttermilk it is always brought to the table straight from the oven and eaten with fork or spoon as a side dish.

1½ cups boiling water
1 cup cornmeal
1 tablespoon margarine or butter, softened
3 eggs, separated
1 cup buttermilk
1 teaspoon salt
1 teaspoon sugar
1 teaspoon baking powder
¼ teaspoon baking soda

Heat oven to 375°. Stir boiling water into cornmeal in 2-quart bowl; continue stirring until lukewarm. Stir in 1 tablespoon margarine and the egg yolks until blended. Stir in buttermilk, salt, sugar, baking powder and baking soda. Beat egg whites just until soft peaks form; fold into batter. Pour into greased 2-quart casserole. Bake until knife inserted near center comes out clean, 45 to 50 minutes. *8 servings.*

Popovers, Peach Preserves (page 64)

Hush Puppies

During colonial times, breads with cornmeal were as common in New England as in the South. Southern settlers continued to rely on corn breads in various forms: hoecakes, ashcakes, corn pone, corn dodgers and, the most fanciful, hush puppies. Southern folklore says that hush puppies got their name because they were tossed to quiet the dogs that men and boys took with them on fishing trips. To this day, a Carolina seafood dinner or Mississippi catfish fry is not complete unless these onion-flavored bits of deep-fried "pone" are served.

Vegetable oil
1½ cups cornmeal
½ cup all-purpose flour
¼ cup shortening
1 cup milk
2 tablespoons finely chopped onion
2 teaspoons baking powder
1 teaspoon sugar
1 teaspoon salt
½ teaspoon baking soda
¼ to ½ teaspoon ground red pepper
1 egg

Heat oil (1 inch) in Dutch oven to 375°. Mix remaining ingredients. Drop by teaspoonfuls into hot oil. Fry, turning once, until golden brown, about 1 minute; drain. *About 4 dozen hush puppies.*

Sour Cream Coffee Cake

Rich sour cream coffee cakes have a long tradition among Jewish immigrants. This recipe is an all-time favorite among recipe collectors.

Cinnamon Filling (below)
1½ cups sugar
¾ cup margarine or butter, softened
1½ teaspoons vanilla
3 eggs
3 cups all-purpose or whole wheat flour
1½ teaspoons baking powder
1½ teaspoons baking soda
¾ teaspoon salt
1½ cups dairy sour cream
½ cup powdered sugar
¼ teaspoon vanilla
1 to 2 teaspoons milk

Heat oven to 325°. Grease tube pan, 10 × 4 inches, or 12-cup bundt cake pan. Prepare Cinnamon Filling; reserve. Beat sugar, margarine, vanilla and eggs in 2½-quart bowl on medium speed, scraping bowl occasionally, 2 minutes. Beat in flour, baking powder, baking soda and salt alternately with sour cream on low speed. Spread ⅓ of the batter (about 2 cups) in pan; sprinkle with ⅓ of the filling (about ⅓ cup). Repeat 2 times. Bake until wooden pick inserted near center comes out clean, about 1 hour. Cool 20 minutes; remove from pan. Mix remaining ingredients until smooth and of desired consistency; drizzle over coffee cake. *16 servings.*

Cinnamon Filling

Mix ½ cup brown sugar, ½ cup finely chopped nuts and 1½ teaspoons ground cinnamon.

German Apple Pancakes

Seattle residents associate these puffy oven pancakes with a family restaurant that was an area institution until the 1950s. The Seattle ancestors were known as Dutch Babies, a name by which many still call these pancakes today.

¾ cup all-purpose flour
¾ cup milk
½ teaspoon salt
4 eggs
¼ cup margarine or butter
2 medium all-purpose apples, thinly sliced
¼ cup sugar
¼ teaspoon ground cinnamon

Heat oven to 400°. Place 2 round pans, 9 × 1½ inches, in oven. Beat flour, milk, salt and eggs on medium speed 1 minute. Remove pans from oven. Place 2 tablespoons margarine in each pan; rotate pans until margarine is melted and coats sides of pans.

Arrange half of the apple slices in each pan; divide batter evenly between pans. Mix sugar and cinnamon; sprinkle 2 tablespoons sugar mixture over batter in each pan. Bake until puffed and golden brown, 20 to 25 minutes. *4 servings.*

Buckwheat Pancakes

Dutch settlers cultivated fields of buckwheat in the Hudson River valley and introduced New Englanders to the pleasures of buckwheat cakes for breakfast. The practice spread to the South and is immortalized in the song "Dixie" with the words "There's buckwheat cakes and Indian batter . . ." Now buckwheat is largely grown in the Northwest, and you can find it in specialty food stores for this simplified version of an old-time treat.

---

1 egg
½ cup buckwheat flour
½ cup whole wheat flour
1 cup milk
1 tablespoon sugar
2 tablespoons vegetable oil or shortening, melted
3 teaspoons baking powder
½ teaspoon salt
   Whole bran or wheat germ, if desired

Beat egg with hand beater until fluffy; beat in remaining ingredients, except bran, just until smooth. Grease heated griddle if necessary. (To test griddle, sprinkle with few drops water. If bubbles skitter around, heat is just right.)

For each pancake, pour about 3 tablespoons batter from tip of large spoon or from pitcher onto hot griddle. Cook pancakes until puffed and dry around edges. Sprinkle each pancake with 1 teaspoon whole bran. Turn and cook other sides until golden brown. *Ten 4-inch pancakes.*

Blueberry Pancakes: Substitute 1 cup all-purpose flour for the buckwheat and whole wheat flours. Decrease milk to ¾ cup. Stir in ½ cup fresh or frozen (thawed and well drained) blueberries.

Boston Brown Bread

Using the familiar English plum pudding as a guide, early Yankee housewives used cornmeal along with rye and wheat flour in this moist and flavorful steamed bread. These traditionally round-shaped loaves were served with plenty of butter and often accompanied Saturday night's Boston Baked Beans (page 34).

---

1 cup all-purpose or rye flour
1 cup cornmeal
1 cup whole wheat flour
1 cup raisins, if desired
2 cups buttermilk
¾ cup molasses
2 teaspoons baking soda
1 teaspoon salt

Grease four 19- or 16-ounce cans, each about 2 cups.* Beat all ingredients in 3-quart bowl on low speed, scraping bowl constantly, 30 seconds. Beat on medium speed, scraping bowl constantly, 30 seconds longer. Pour into cans, filling each about ⅔ full. Cover each tightly with aluminum foil.

Place cans on rack in Dutch oven or steamer; pour boiling water into pan to level of rack. Cover pan. Keep water boiling over low heat until wooden pick inserted in center comes out clean, about 2½ hours. (Add boiling water during steaming if necessary.) Remove cans from pan; immediately unmold breads. Serve warm. *4 loaves.*

*Use only unlined cans from heat-processed soups or vegetables.

Potato Doughnuts

*Dutch housewives in New Amsterdam — later New York — prided themselves on three kinds of fried cakes. "Heaped-up platters" of doughnuts, crullers and fried cakes known as **olykoeks** were described by Washington Irving in his **Legend of Sleepy Hollow** as ". . . one of the ample charms of a genuine Dutch tea-table."*

---

1 package active dry yeast
1½ cups warm water (105 to 115°)
⅔ cup sugar
1½ teaspoons salt
⅔ cup shortening
2 eggs
1 cup lukewarm mashed cooked potatoes
6 to 7 cups all-purpose flour
   Vegetable oil
   Glaze (below)

Dissolve yeast in warm water in 3-quart bowl. Stir in sugar, salt, shortening, eggs, potatoes and 3 cups of the flour. Beat until smooth. Mix in enough remaining flour to make dough easy to handle. Turn dough onto well-floured surface; knead until smooth and elastic, about 5 minutes. Place in greased bowl; turn greased side up. Cover tightly; refrigerate at least 8 hours.

Punch down dough. Pat to ¾-inch thickness on lightly floured surface. Cut with floured 2½-inch doughnut cutter. Cover; let rise in warm place until indentation remains when touched, 45 to 60 minutes.

Heat oil (3 to 4 inches) in deep fryer or Dutch oven to 375°. Fry doughnuts until golden brown, 1 to 2 minutes on each side; drain. Dip warm doughnuts in Glaze. *About 2½ dozen doughnuts.*

Glaze

Mix 3 cups powdered sugar and ½ cup boiling water until smooth.

Philadelphia Sticky Buns

Philadelphia Sticky Buns

*Generations of Philadelphians have enjoyed these special cinnamon buns. Descendants of the snail-shaped buns, **schnecken**, popular with the Pennsylvania Dutch settlers, their uniqueness comes from nuts and raisins in the filling and an extra stickiness that is not found in other popular American cinnamon rolls.*

1 package regular or quick-acting active dry yeast
½ cup warm water (105 to 115°)
½ cup lukewarm milk (scalded then cooled)
⅓ cup granulated sugar
⅓ cup shortening, margarine or butter, softened
1 teaspoon salt
1 egg
3½ to 4 cups all-purpose flour
1 cup packed brown sugar
½ cup margarine or butter
¼ cup corn syrup
2 tablespoons margarine or butter, softened
  Filling (right)

Dissolve yeast in warm water in 2½-quart bowl. Stir in milk, granulated sugar, shortening, salt, egg and 2 cups of the flour. Beat until smooth. Mix in enough remaining flour to make dough easy to handle. Turn dough onto lightly floured surface; knead until smooth and elastic, about 5 minutes. Place in greased bowl; turn greased side up. Cover; let rise in warm place until double, about 1½ hours. (Dough is ready if indentation remains when touched.)

Heat brown sugar and ½ cup margarine to boiling, stirring constantly; remove from heat. Stir in corn syrup; cool 5 minutes. Pour into greased rectangular pan, 13 × 9 × 2 inches.

Punch down dough. Flatten with hands or rolling pin into rectangle, 15 × 10 inches, on lightly floured surface; spread with 2 tablespoons margarine. Sprinkle Filling evenly over margarine. Roll up tightly, beginning at 15-inch side. Pinch edge of dough into roll to seal well. Stretch roll to make even. Cut into fifteen 1-inch slices. Place slightly apart in pan. Let rise until double, about 40 minutes.

Heat oven to 375°. Bake until golden brown, 30 to 35 minutes. Immediately invert pan on heatproof tray. Let pan remain a minute so caramel can drizzle over rolls. Spoon any caramel from tray over rolls. *15 rolls.*

Filling

Mix ½ cup chopped nuts, ½ cup raisins and 1½ teaspoons ground cinnamon.

Sourdough Bread

On the American frontier, every traveler carried a crock of sourdough starter for bread and flapjacks. Today, however, Sourdough Bread is almost synonymous with San Francisco. As this recipe proves, it **is** possible to bake a good loaf at home. However, without a humidity-controlled oven, it's impossible to duplicate exactly the crusty loaves sold along Fisherman's Wharf.

1 cup Sourdough Starter (right)
2½ cups all-purpose flour
2 cups warm water (105 to 115°)
3¾ to 4¼ cups all-purpose flour
3 tablespoons sugar
3 tablespoons vegetable oil
1 teaspoon salt
¼ teaspoon baking soda
  Cold water

Mix 1 cup Sourdough Starter, 2½ cups flour and 2 cups warm water in 3-quart glass bowl with wooden spoon until smooth. Cover; let stand in warm, draft-free place 8 hours.

Add 3¾ cups flour, the sugar, oil, salt and baking soda to mixture in bowl. Stir with wooden spoon until dough is smooth and flour is completely absorbed. (Dough should be just firm enough to gather into ball. If necessary, gradually add remaining ½ cup flour, stirring until all flour is absorbed.)

Turn dough onto heavily floured surface; knead until smooth and elastic, about 10 minutes. Place in greased bowl; turn greased side up. Cover; let rise in warm place until double, about 1½ hours. (Dough is ready if indentation remains when touched.)

Punch down dough; divide into halves. Shape each half into round, slightly flat loaf. Do not tear dough by pulling. Place loaves in opposite corners of greased cookie sheet. Make three ¼-inch-deep slashes in each loaf. Let rise until double, about 45 minutes.

Heat oven to 375°. Brush loaves with cold water. Place cookie sheet in center of oven. Cookie sheet should not touch sides of oven. Bake, brushing occasionally with water, until loaves sound hollow when tapped, about 50 minutes. Remove from cookie sheet; cool on wire racks. *2 loaves.*

Sourdough Starter

1 teaspoon active dry yeast
¼ cup warm water (105 to 115°)
¾ cup milk
1 cup all-purpose flour

Dissolve yeast in warm water in 3-quart glass bowl. Stir in milk. Gradually stir in flour. Beat until smooth. Cover with towel or cheesecloth; let stand in warm, draft-free place until starter begins to ferment, about 24 hours (bubbles will appear on surface of starter). If fermentation has not begun after 24 hours, discard and begin again. If fermentation has begun, stir well; cover tightly with plastic wrap and return to warm, draft-free place. Let stand until foamy, 2 to 3 days.

When starter has become foamy, stir well; pour into 1-quart crock or glass jar with tight cover. Store in refrigerator. Starter is ready to use when a clear liquid has risen to top. Stir before using. Use 1 cup starter in recipe; reserve remaining starter. Add ¾ cup milk and ¾ cup all-purpose flour to reserved starter. Cover and store at room temperature until bubbles appear, about 12 hours; refrigerate.

Use starter regularly, every week to 10 days. If volume of baked breads begins to decrease, dissolve 1 teaspoon active dry yeast in ¼ cup warm water. Stir in ½ cup milk, ¾ cup all-purpose flour and the remaining starter.

Mixed Berry Jam

The ease with which the just-picked freshness of straw-berries and raspberries could be turned into glisten-ing jam popularized recipes for uncooked fruit jams in the 1960s.

1 cup crushed strawberries (about 1 pint whole
   berries)
1 cup crushed raspberries (about 1 pint whole
   berries)
4 cups sugar
½ teaspoon grated lemon peel
1 tablespoon lemon juice
1 pouch (3 ounces) liquid fruit pectin

Mix berries and sugar; let stand at room temperature, stirring occasionally, until sugar is dissolved, about 10 minutes. Mix in lemon peel, lemon juice and pectin; stir until slightly thickened, 3 to 5 minutes. Spoon mixture into freezer containers, leaving ½-inch headspace. Seal immediately. Let stand at room temperature 24 hours. (To store, refrigerate no longer than 3 weeks or freeze no longer than 1 year. Thaw before serving.) *About 5 half-pints jam.*

Peach Preserves

Catch peaches at the peak of their growing season — between May and October — to capture their sunny goodness in this heirloom recipe. A cup of tea and a slice of warm, homemade bread spread with Peach Preserves is an old remedy for many small troubles.

4 pounds peaches, peeled and sliced (about 8 cups)
6 cups sugar
¼ cup lemon juice

Toss peaches and sugar. Cover and refrigerate at least 12 hours but no longer than 24 hours.

Heat peach mixture to boiling, stirring constantly. Rapidly boil uncovered 20 minutes. Stir in lemon juice. Boil uncovered 10 minutes longer. Immediately pour mixture into hot jars, leaving ¼-inch headspace. Wipe rims of jars. Seal and process in boiling water bath 15 minutes. *About 6 half-pints preserves.*

Corn Relish

Colorful Corn Relish often teamed with rosy pickled beets could be counted on to brighten the winter dinner tables in corn belt farm kitchens.

9 ears corn
1½ cups sugar
3 tablespoons all-purpose flour
2 tablespoons pickling or uniodized salt
2 teaspoons dry mustard
1 teaspoon ground turmeric
3 cups white vinegar
3 medium onions, chopped
2 red peppers, chopped
1 green pepper, chopped
1 small head green cabbage, chopped

Place corn in Dutch oven; add enough cold water to cover. Heat to boiling. Boil uncovered 3 minutes. Drain water from corn; cool. Cut enough kernels from corn to measure 5 cups.

Mix sugar, flour, salt, mustard and turmeric in Dutch oven; stir in vinegar. Heat to boiling; reduce heat. Add corn and remaining vegetables. Simmer uncovered 25 minutes. Immediately pack mixture in hot jars, leaving ¼-inch headspace. Wipe rims of jars. Seal and process in boiling water bath 15 minutes. *5 or 6 pints relish.*

Pineapple Pickles

Hawaiian cooks contributed to America's heritage of "putting up" pickles by turning pineapple and other exotic fruits into jewel-colored pickles and chut-neys. Gingerroot, a flavor found repeatedly in Poly-nesian cooking, blends with cinnamon and cloves in this special recipe.

3 large pineapples (about 5 pounds each)
2 tablespoons whole cloves
3 sticks cinnamon, broken into pieces
1 thin slice gingerroot, coarsely chopped
5 cups sugar
1½ cups cider vinegar

Cut pineapples crosswise into 1-inch slices. Cut off rind, remove eyes and core. Cut pineapple into 1-inch pieces; drain thoroughly.

Tie cloves, cinnamon and gingerroot in cheese-cloth bag. Heat cheesecloth bag, sugar and vinegar to boiling in Dutch oven, stirring occasionally. Boil uncovered 5 minutes; reduce heat. Add pineapple. Simmer uncovered 1 hour, stirring occasionally. Remove cheese-cloth bag. Immediately pack mixture loosely in hot jars, leaving ¼-inch headspace. Wipe rims of jars. Seal and process in boiling water bath 10 minutes. Let stand at least 2 weeks before serving. *5 pints pickles.*

Watermelon Pickles

Jars of these pickles, translucent pale green with an occasional blush of pink, are sought by eager customers at church bazaars in small towns across this country.

¼ cup pickling or uniodized salt
8 cups cold water
4 quarts 1-inch cubes pared watermelon rind
2 tablespoons whole cloves
3 sticks cinnamon, broken into pieces
1 piece gingerroot
9 cups sugar
8 cups cider vinegar

Dissolve salt in cold water; pour over water-melon rind. Stir in additional water, if necessary, to cover rind. Let stand in cool place 8 hours.

Drain rind; cover with cold water. Heat to boiling. Cook uncovered just until tender, 10 to 15 minutes; drain. Tie cloves, cinnamon and gingerroot in cheesecloth bag. Heat cheese-cloth bag, sugar and vinegar to boiling in Dutch oven, stirring occasionally. Boil uncovered 5 minutes; reduce heat. Add rind. Simmer uncovered 1 hour, stirring occasionally. Remove cheesecloth bag. Immediately pack mixture in hot jars, leaving ¼-inch headspace. Wipe rims of jars. Seal and process in boiling water bath 10 minutes. *7 to 8 pints pickles.*

Watermelon Pickles

Desserts

Lemon-filled Coconut Cake

Cakes like this one were known as "refrigerator" cakes in the 1940s. America's growing prosperity made it possible for nearly everyone to afford one of the new electric refrigerators, giving homemakers a dependable place to store these creamy chilled desserts.

Lemon Filling (right)
2½ cups all-purpose flour
1⅔ cups granulated sugar
⅔ cup shortening
1¼ cups milk
3½ teaspoons baking powder
1 teaspoon salt
1 teaspoon vanilla
5 egg whites
1 cup flaked or shredded coconut
1 cup chilled whipping cream
¼ cup powdered sugar

Prepare Lemon Filling; press plastic wrap onto filling. Refrigerate until set, about 1 hour.

Heat oven to 350°. Grease and flour 2 round pans, 8 or 9 × 1½ inches. Beat flour, granulated sugar, shortening, milk, baking powder, salt and vanilla in 3-quart bowl on low speed, scraping bowl constantly, 30 seconds. Beat on high speed, scraping bowl occasionally, 2 minutes. Beat in egg whites on high speed, scraping bowl occasionally, 2 minutes. Stir in coconut. Pour into pans.

Bake until wooden pick inserted in center comes out clean or top springs back when touched lightly, 30 to 35 minutes. Cool 10 minutes; remove from pans. Cool completely.

Beat whipping cream and powdered sugar in chilled 1½-quart bowl until stiff. Fill layers with Lemon Filling, frost with whipped cream and garnish with shredded coconut, if desired; refrigerate. Immediately refrigerate any remaining cake.

Lemon Filling

¾ cup sugar
3 tablespoons cornstarch
¼ teaspoon salt
¾ cup water
1 tablespoon margarine or butter
1 teaspoon finely shredded lemon peel
⅓ cup lemon juice
2 to 4 drops yellow food color, if desired

Mix sugar, cornstarch and salt in 1½-quart saucepan. Gradually stir in water. Cook over medium heat, stirring constantly, until mixture thickens and boils. Boil and stir 5 minutes; remove from heat. Stir in margarine and lemon peel until margarine is melted. Gradually stir in lemon juice and food color.

Lemon-filled Coconut Cake, Key Lime Pie (page 74)

Red Devils Food Cake

Red Devils Food Cake

"Devilishly good" is how some described the moist, reddish-brown chocolate cake that first appeared on midwestern tables in the 1880s. Thought of as the finest American chocolate layer cake because of its richness, the red color — partly from baking soda used as leavening — was highlighted by a creamy white frosting.

1⅔ cups all-purpose flour
 1 cup granulated sugar
 ½ cup packed brown sugar
 ½ cup shortening
1½ cups buttermilk
1½ teaspoons baking soda
 1 teaspoon salt
 1 teaspoon vanilla
 ½ teaspoon red food color
 2 squares (1 ounce each) unsweetened chocolate, melted and cooled
 2 eggs

Heat oven to 350°. Grease and flour 2 round pans, 8 or 9 × 1½ inches, or rectangular pan, 13 × 9 × 2 inches. Beat all ingredients on low speed, scraping bowl constantly, 30 seconds. Beat on high speed, scraping bowl occasionally, 3 minutes. Pour into pan(s).

Bake until wooden pick inserted in center comes out clean, layers 30 to 35 minutes, rectangle 35 to 40 minutes. Cool layers 10 minutes; remove from pans. Cool completely. Fill and frost layers or frost top of rectangle with Creamy Vanilla Frosting (below) if desired.

Creamy Vanilla Frosting

 3 cups powdered sugar
 ⅓ cup margarine or butter, softened
1½ teaspoons vanilla
 About 2 tablespoons milk

Mix powdered sugar and margarine. Stir in vanilla and milk; beat until smooth and of spreading consistency.

Red Devils Food Cake

German Chocolate Cake

Although a relative newcomer to the dessert scene, German Chocolate Cake was inspired by the sweet chocolate bar developed nearly one hundred years earlier in 1852 by a man named Samuel German, an employee of one of America's leading chocolate manufacturers. Although a version of the cake was brought to Texas in the early 1800s, this is the grass roots recipe that swept the country in the 1950s to become one of America's best-loved chocolate cakes.

½ cup boiling water
1 bar (4 ounces) sweet cooking chocolate
2 cups sugar
1 cup margarine or butter, softened
4 egg yolks
1 teaspoon vanilla
2½ cups cake flour
1 teaspoon baking soda
1 teaspoon salt
1 cup buttermilk
4 egg whites, stiffly beaten
  Coconut-Pecan Frosting (right)

Heat oven to 350°. Grease 2 square pans, 8 × 8 × 2 or 9 × 9 × 2 inches, or 3 round pans, 8 or 9 × 1½ inches. Line bottoms of pans with waxed paper. Pour boiling water on chocolate, stirring until chocolate is melted; cool.

Mix sugar and margarine in 3-quart bowl until light and fluffy. Beat in egg yolks, one at a time. Beat in chocolate and vanilla on low speed. Mix in flour, baking soda and salt alternately with buttermilk, beating after each addition until batter is smooth. Fold in egg whites. Pour into pans.

Bake until wooden pick inserted in center comes out clean, 8-inch squares 45 to 50 minutes, 9-inch squares 40 to 45 minutes, 8-inch rounds 35 to 40 minutes, 9-inch rounds 30 to 35 minutes; cool. Fill layers and frost top of cake with Coconut-Pecan Frosting.

Coconut-Pecan Frosting

1 cup sugar
½ cup margarine or butter
1 cup evaporated milk
1 teaspoon vanilla
3 egg yolks
1⅓ cups flaked coconut
1 cup chopped pecans

Mix sugar, margarine, milk, vanilla and egg yolks in saucepan. Cook over medium heat, stirring occasionally, until thick, about 12 minutes. Stir in coconut and pecans. Beat until of spreading consistency.

Dinette Cake

In the 1890s, this popular cake was called One-Egg Cake. During the 1920s and 1930s, it was promoted as Emergency or Lazy Day Cake. Reflecting changing times, by the 1940s the cake was referred to as Busy Day Cake and became Kitchenette Cake in the 1950s.

1¼ cups all-purpose flour or 1½ cups cake flour
1 cup sugar
1½ teaspoons baking powder
½ teaspoon salt
¾ cup milk
⅓ cup shortening
1 egg
1 teaspoon vanilla

Heat oven to 350°. Grease and flour square pan, 8 × 8 × 2 or 9 × 9 × 2 inches, or round pan, 9 × 1½ inches. Beat all ingredients in large bowl on low speed, scraping bowl constantly, 30 seconds. Beat on high speed, scraping bowl occasionally, 3 minutes. Pour into pan.

Bake until wooden pick inserted in center comes out clean, square 35 to 40 minutes, round about 35 minutes. Cool 10 minutes; remove from pan. Cool completely. Frost with Caramel Frosting (page 71) or other frosting if desired (cut recipe in half).

Boston Cream Pie

A simple yellow cake gets special treatment in what is probably New England's most famous dessert. First baked in a pie pan, which accounts for the unlikely name of Boston Cream Pie, the cake was split and layered with Cream Filling. Boston's Parker House hotel is credited with glazing the cake with chocolate — the variation that has become the nation's favorite.

1¼ cups all-purpose flour or 1½ cups cake flour
 1 cup sugar
1½ teaspoons baking powder
 ½ teaspoon salt
 ¾ cup milk
 ⅓ cup shortening
 1 egg
 1 teaspoon vanilla
  Cream Filling (below)
  Chocolate Glaze (right)

Heat oven to 350°. Grease and flour round pan, 9 × 1½ inches. Beat all ingredients except filling and glaze on low speed, scraping bowl constantly, 30 seconds. Beat on high speed, scraping bowl occasionally, 3 minutes. Pour into pan.

Bake until wooden pick inserted in center comes out clean, about 35 minutes. Cool 10 minutes; remove from pan. Cool completely.

Prepare Cream Filling; cool. Split cake horizontally into halves. Fill layers with filling. Spread top of cake with Chocolate Glaze; refrigerate. Immediately refrigerate any remaining dessert.

Cream Filling

 ⅓ cup sugar
 2 tablespoons cornstarch
 ⅛ teaspoon salt
1½ cups milk
 2 egg yolks, slightly beaten
 2 teaspoons vanilla

Mix sugar, cornstarch and salt in 2-quart saucepan. Mix milk and egg yolks; gradually stir into sugar mixture. Cook over medium heat, stirring constantly, until mixture thickens and boils. Boil and stir 1 minute; remove from heat. Stir in vanilla.

Chocolate Glaze

 3 tablespoons margarine or butter
 3 squares (1 ounce each) unsweetened chocolate
 1 cup powdered sugar
 ¾ teaspoon vanilla
  About 2 tablespoons hot water

Heat margarine and chocolate in 1-quart saucepan over low heat, stirring constantly, until chocolate is melted; remove from heat. Stir in powdered sugar and vanilla. Stir in water, 1 teaspoon at a time, until smooth and of desired consistency.

Raspberry Jam Cake

Raspberry Jam Cake

Pioneer women relied on the fruits and nuts they found growing wild to flavor their baking specialties. Long a staple of the hill and mountain country throughout the Appalachian mountain states, spice-laden jam cakes were "good keepers" for when friends stopped by, particularly at Christmastime. Topping the cake with Caramel Frosting is a time-honored Southern custom.

1 cup margarine or butter, softened
½ cup granulated sugar
½ cup packed brown sugar
4 eggs
1 jar (10 ounces) red raspberry preserves
   (about 1 cup)
3¼ cups all-purpose flour
1 teaspoon baking powder
1 teaspoon baking soda
1 teaspoon ground nutmeg
1 teaspoon ground cinnamon
½ teaspoon salt
¼ teaspoon ground cloves
1 cup buttermilk
1 cup chopped pecans
   Caramel Frosting (right)

Heat oven to 350°. Grease and flour tube pan, 10 × 4 inches. Beat margarine and sugars in 3-quart bowl on medium speed, scraping bowl constantly, until blended. Beat on high speed 1 minute. Beat in eggs and preserves until well blended. (Mixture will appear curdled.) Beat in flour, baking powder, baking soda, nutmeg, cinnamon, salt and cloves alternately with buttermilk, beginning and ending with flour mixture, until well blended. Stir in pecans. Pour into pan.

Bake until wooden pick inserted in center comes out clean and top springs back when touched lightly, 70 to 75 minutes. Cool 10 minutes; remove from pan. Cool completely. Frost with Caramel Frosting.

Caramel Frosting

½ cup margarine or butter
1 cup packed brown sugar
¼ cup milk
2 cups powdered sugar

Heat margarine in 2-quart saucepan until melted. Stir in brown sugar. Heat to boiling, stirring constantly. Boil and stir over low heat 2 minutes; stir in milk. Heat to boiling; remove from heat. Cool to lukewarm. Gradually stir in powdered sugar; beat until smooth and of spreading consistency. If frosting becomes too stiff, stir in additional milk, 1 teaspoon at a time.

Pound Cake

Because pound cakes taste even better a day or two after baking, homemakers in great-grandmother's day depended on the cake's delectable goodness when company unexpectedly came calling. The original proportions of a pound each of flour, sugar, butter and eggs have changed over the years and today's recipes assure success by using both baking powder and the electric mixer.

2¾ cups sugar
1¼ cups margarine or butter, softened
1 teaspoon vanilla
5 eggs
3 cups all-purpose flour
1 teaspoon baking powder
¼ teaspoon salt
1 cup evaporated milk

Heat oven to 350°. Grease and flour 12-cup bundt cake pan or tube pan, 10 × 4 inches. Beat sugar, margarine, vanilla and eggs in 3-quart bowl on low speed, scraping bowl constantly, 30 seconds. Beat on high speed, scraping bowl occasionally, 5 minutes. Beat in flour, baking powder and salt alternately with milk on low speed. Pour into pan.

Bake until wooden pick inserted in center comes out clean, 70 to 80 minutes. Cool 20 minutes; remove from pan.

Almond Pound Cake: Substitute almond extract for the vanilla.

Lemon Pound Cake: Substitute lemon extract for the vanilla and fold 2 to 3 teaspoons grated lemon peel into batter.

Orange-Coconut Pound Cake: Fold 1 can (3½ ounces) flaked coconut (1⅓ cups) and 2 to 3 tablespoons shredded orange peel into batter.

Orange Chiffon Cake

Introduced by General Mills in 1948, chiffon cake was called "the cake discovery of the century!" Its inventor, Harry Baker, a California insurance sales-man, had kept his recipe a secret for twenty years before sharing it with his "friend" Betty Crocker. The cake's mystery ingredient — new to cakemaking — was salad or cooking oil, making chiffon cake "light as angel food, rich as butter cake and easy to make."

2 cups all-purpose flour or 2¼ cups cake flour
1½ cups sugar
3 teaspoons baking powder
1 teaspoon salt
¾ cup cold water
½ cup vegetable oil
2 tablespoons grated orange peel
7 egg yolks (with all-purpose flour) or
   5 egg yolks (with cake flour)
1 cup egg whites (about 8)
½ teaspoon cream of tartar

Heat oven to 325°. Mix flour, sugar, baking powder and salt in 1½-quart bowl. Beat in water, oil, orange peel and egg yolks with spoon until smooth. Beat egg whites and cream of tartar in 3-quart bowl until stiff peaks form. Gradually pour egg yolk mixture over beaten egg whites, folding with rubber spatula just until blended. Pour into ungreased tube pan, 10 × 4 inches.

Bake until top springs back when touched lightly, about 1¼ hours. Invert pan on heat-proof funnel; let hang until cake is cold. Remove from pan. Frost with Creamy Orange Frosting (below) if desired.

Creamy Orange Frosting

3 cups powdered sugar
⅓ cup margarine or butter, softened
   About 2 tablespoons orange juice
2 teaspoons grated orange peel

Mix powdered sugar and margarine. Stir in orange juice; beat until smooth and of spreading consistency. Stir in orange peel.

Chocolate Angel Food Cake

Another cake with mysterious origins is the angel food, which achieved its height of appeal in the nineteenth century. It is an American original. Frugality — a way to use leftover egg whites — is one notion about why the cake was invented. There is some evidence that a St. Louis restaurateur invented this light, airy cake with the addition of a "magic ingredient" called cream of tartar. Today, the angel food has come back into its own because it is low in cholesterol and calories.

1½ cups powdered sugar
¾ cup cake flour
¼ cup cocoa
1½ cups egg whites (about 12)
1½ teaspoons cream of tartar
1 cup granulated sugar
1½ teaspoons vanilla
¼ teaspoon salt

Heat oven to 375°. Mix powdered sugar, flour and cocoa. Beat egg whites and cream of tartar in 3-quart bowl on medium speed until foamy. Beat in granulated sugar on high speed, 2 tablespoons at a time, adding vanilla and salt with the last addition of sugar; continue beating until stiff and glossy. Do not underbeat.

Sprinkle flour mixture, ¼ cup at a time, over meringue, folding in just until flour mixture disappears. Spread batter in ungreased tube pan, 10 × 4 inches. Cut gently through batter with metal spatula.

Bake until cracks feel dry and top springs back when touched lightly, 30 to 35 minutes. Invert pan on heatproof funnel; let hang until cake is cold. Remove from pan. Frost top and side of cake with Mocha Fluff or spread top with Vanilla Glaze (right) if desired.

Mocha Fluff

1 cup powdered sugar
¼ cup cocoa
1 teaspoon powdered instant coffee (dry)
2 cups chilled whipping cream

Beat all ingredients in chilled 2½-quart bowl until stiff. (When using this frosting, immediately refrigerate any remaining cake.)

Vanilla Glaze

2 cups powdered sugar
⅓ cup margarine or butter, melted
1½ teaspoons vanilla
2 to 4 tablespoons hot water

Mix powdered sugar, margarine and vanilla. Stir in water, 1 tablespoon at a time, until smooth and of desired consistency.

Angel Food Cake: Omit cocoa and increase flour to 1 cup. Add ½ teaspoon almond extract with the last addition of sugar. Spread top of cake with Vanilla Glaze if desired.

Coconut Angel Food Cake: Omit cocoa and increase flour to 1 cup. Add ½ teaspoon almond extract with the last addition of sugar. Fold in 1 cup shredded coconut, ½ cup at a time, after folding in flour mixture. Spread top of cake with Vanilla Glaze if desired.

Black Bottom Pie

Black Bottom Pies have been special-occasion pies in the South since the turn of the century. This triple-tiered fantasy of rich chocolate, rum-flavored custard and whipping cream fills a tempting Gingersnap Crust

---

Gingersnap Crust (right)
½ cup sugar
2 tablespoons cornstarch
¼ teaspoon salt
2 cups milk
3 egg yolks
1 teaspoon vanilla
1 envelope unflavored gelatin
¼ cup cold water
1 to 2 tablespoons rum or 1 teaspoon rum flavoring
3 squares (1 ounce each) semisweet chocolate, melted and cooled
3 egg whites
¼ teaspoon cream of tartar
⅓ cup sugar
1 cup chilled whipping cream
2 tablespoons powdered sugar

Bake Gingersnap Crust; cool. Mix ½ cup sugar, the cornstarch and salt in 2-quart saucepan. Mix milk and egg yolks; gradually stir into sugar mixture. Cook over medium heat, stirring constantly, until mixture thickens and boils. Boil and stir 1 minute. Stir in vanilla. Remove 1 cup custard; reserve.

Sprinkle gelatin on cold water to soften; stir into custard in pan until gelatin is dissolved. Stir in rum. Refrigerate, stirring occasionally, until mixture mounds when dropped from a spoon, about 10 minutes.

Mix chocolate and the 1 cup of reserved custard; pour into crust. Beat egg whites and cream of tartar in 2½-quart bowl until foamy. Beat in ⅓ cup sugar, 1 tablespoon at a time; continue beating until stiff and glossy. Do not underbeat. Fold chilled custard mixture into meringue; spread over chocolate mixture. Refrigerate until set, at least 3 hours.

Beat whipping cream and powdered sugar in chilled 1½-quart bowl until stiff. Spread over pie. Sprinkle with ground nutmeg if desired. Immediately refrigerate any remaining pie.

Gingersnap Crust

Heat oven to 350°. Mix 1½ cups crushed gingersnaps (about 22) and ¼ cup margarine or butter, melted. Press firmly and evenly against bottom and side of ungreased pie plate, 9 × 1¼ inches. Bake 10 minutes.

Key Lime Pie

Backyard gardens are the only fresh source today for the legendary yellow Key limes from which the equally notable Key Lime Pies are made. Thank goodness Persian limes and lemons are suitable substitutes. This delectable pie, which also owes its existence to the invention of sweetened condensed milk, is a cool and creamy taste of the tropics.

---

1 can (14 ounces) sweetened condensed milk
1 tablespoon grated lemon peel
½ teaspoon grated lime peel
¼ cup lemon juice
¼ cup lime juice
3 or 4 drops green food color
3 eggs, separated
¼ teaspoon cream of tartar
9-inch baked pie shell

Mix milk, lemon and lime peel, lemon and lime juices and food color. Beat egg yolks slightly; stir in milk mixture. Beat egg whites and cream of tartar in 2½-quart bowl until stiff and glossy. Fold egg yolk mixture into egg whites; mound in pie shell. Refrigerate until set, at least 2 hours. Garnish with sweetened whipped cream and lime slices if desired. Immediately refrigerate any remaining pie.

Fresh Fruit Tart

Fresh Fruit Tart

Fresh and fabulous desserts that are easy on the cook became the byword of busy women in the 1960s. Fruit tarts, like this one, extended the use of a piece of kitchen equipment that became commonplace in American homes at this time, the pizza pan.

Cookie Crust (right)
1 package (3 ounces) cream cheese, softened
⅓ cup sugar
1 teaspoon vanilla
1 cup chilled whipping cream
1 cup blueberries
1 cup strawberries, cut into halves
5 apricots, cut into fourths
1 kiwifruit, sliced
¼ to ½ cup apple jelly

Bake Cookie Crust; cool. Beat cream cheese, sugar and vanilla in 1½-quart bowl on low speed until smooth. Beat in whipping cream on low speed until blended; beat on medium speed until stiff peaks form. Spread over crust to within ¼ inch of edge. Arrange fruits in circles on crust. Heat jelly over low heat, stirring constantly, until melted; brush over fruit. Refrigerate at least 2 hours. Immediately refrigerate any remaining tart. *12 to 14 servings.*

Cookie Crust

1½ cups all-purpose flour
¼ cup plus 2 tablespoons powdered sugar
¾ cup margarine or butter, softened

Heat oven to 400°. Mix all ingredients with fork until crumbly. Press firmly and evenly against bottom of ungreased 12-inch pizza pan. Bake until light brown, 10 to 15 minutes.

Pies 75

Kentucky Pecan Pie

To someone from the South, nothing compares to pecan pie — except perhaps another variation of this sinfully rich classic! Kentuckians bake their particular specialty using chocolate chips and bourbon at Derby time. Native southern pecans paired with homegrown cane sugar made this pie a matchless creation.

Pastry for 9-inch one-crust pie
²/₃ cup sugar
¹/₃ cup margarine or butter, melted
1 cup corn syrup
2 tablespoons bourbon
½ teaspoon salt
3 eggs
1 cup pecan halves or broken pecans
1 cup semisweet chocolate chips

Heat oven to 375°. Prepare pastry. Beat sugar, margarine, corn syrup, bourbon, salt and eggs with hand beater. Stir in pecans and chocolate chips. Pour into pastry-lined pie plate. Bake until set, 40 to 50 minutes. Refrigerate until chilled, at least 2 hours. Immediately refrigerate any remaining pie.

Brandy Pecan Pie: Decrease corn syrup to ¾ cup. Substitute ¼ cup brandy for the bourbon and omit chocolate chips.

Chocolate Pecan Pie: Melt 2 squares (1 ounce each) unsweetened chocolate with the margarine. Omit bourbon and chocolate chips.

Peanut-Chocolate Chip Pie: Omit bourbon and 1 cup chocolate chips from filling. Substitute 1 cup salted peanuts for the pecans. After baking, sprinkle with ½ cup semisweet chocolate chips. Let stand 30 minutes before refrigerating.

Pecan Pie: Omit bourbon and chocolate chips.

Sweet Potato Pie

Sweet potatoes were introduced to southern colonists by the Indians. The autumn-maturing root vegetable reminded black Americans of the yams that had been a familiar part of their African food heritage. These inventive cooks turned the naturally rich and sweet potatoes into delicious puddings, breads and cakes along with this pie that is synonymous with soul food.

Pastry for 9-inch one-crust pie
2 eggs
¾ cup sugar
1 teaspoon ground cinnamon
½ teaspoon salt
½ teaspoon ground ginger
¼ teaspoon ground cloves
1 can (23 ounces) sweet potatoes, drained and mashed (1¾ to 2 cups)
1 can (12 ounces) evaporated milk

Heat oven to 425°. Prepare pastry. Beat eggs slightly in 2-quart bowl with hand beater; beat in remaining ingredients. Place pastry-lined pie plate on oven rack; pour sweet potato mixture into plate. Bake 15 minutes.

Reduce oven temperature to 350°. Bake until knife inserted in center comes out clean, 45 to 50 minutes. Refrigerate until chilled, at least 4 hours. Serve with sweetened whipped cream if desired. Immediately refrigerate any remaining pie.

Praline Sweet Potato Pie: Decrease second bake time to 35 minutes. Mix ⅓ cup packed brown sugar, ⅓ cup chopped pecans and 1 tablespoon margarine or butter, softened; sprinkle over pie. Bake until knife inserted in center comes out clean, about 10 minutes longer.

Pumpkin Pie: Substitute 1 can (16 ounces) pumpkin for the sweet potatoes.

Honey Walnut Pie

This Golden State rendition of the chess pie classics from the South blends ingredients that came to California with its earliest European settlers. The Franciscan fathers who established the California missions planted the first walnut trees in 1769. Other settlers brought honeybees with them. Honey had become a valuable commodity in the state by 1853, when colonies of bees were sold at auction for as much as $110 each!

Pastry for 9-inch one-crust pie
½ cup packed brown sugar
½ cup corn syrup
½ cup honey
1 tablespoon all-purpose flour
1 tablespoon margarine or butter, melted
1 teaspoon vanilla
¼ teaspoon salt
2 eggs
1½ cups walnut pieces

Heat oven to 350°. Prepare pastry. Beat brown sugar, corn syrup, honey, flour, margarine, vanilla, salt and eggs with hand beater. Stir in walnuts. Pour into pastry-lined pie plate. Bake until set, 45 to 55 minutes. Refrigerate until chilled, at least 2 hours. Immediately refrigerate any remaining pie.

Shoofly Pie

Whether this Pennsylvania Dutch recipe is served at breakfast or for dessert largely depends on the amount of molasses filling, making what is known as either a dry or wet Shoofly Pie. Requiring only the simplest ingredients, "Shooflies" became baking day favorites in late winter when the cream, eggs and dried fruits of the previous summer were in short supply.

Pastry for 9-inch one-crust pie
¾ cup all-purpose flour
½ cup packed brown sugar
3 tablespoons margarine or butter
½ teaspoon salt
½ teaspoon ground cinnamon
¼ teaspoon ground ginger
⅛ teaspoon ground nutmeg
¾ cup hot water
½ teaspoon baking soda
½ cup dark molasses
1 egg yolk, well beaten

Heat oven to 400°. Prepare pastry. Mix flour, brown sugar, margarine, salt, cinnamon, ginger and nutmeg with hands until crumbly. Mix water and baking soda in 1-quart bowl. Stir in molasses and egg yolk. Pour into pastry-lined pie plate. Sprinkle crumbly mixture over molasses mixture. Bake 15 minutes. Reduce oven temperature to 325°. Bake until crust and crumbs are brown, about 20 minutes. Serve warm.

Double Crust Lemon Pie

Lemons are a long-favored flavor for pies among Americans. Double Crust Lemon Pie was first baked in Shaker community kitchens. Anyone who has ever tasted this old-time pie can attest to its heavenly flavor.

---

2 large lemons
2 cups sugar
½ teaspoon salt
Pastry for 9-inch two-crust pie
4 eggs

Grate enough lemon peel to measure 2 teaspoons. Pare lemons, removing all white membrane. Cut lemons into very thin slices. Place slices in bowl; add lemon peel, sugar and salt; reserve.

Heat oven to 425°. Prepare pastry. Beat eggs until foamy. Pour over lemon slices and sugar; mix well. Pour into pastry-lined pie plate. Cover with top crust that has slits cut in it; seal and flute. Brush crust with water and sprinkle with sugar if desired. Cover edge with 2- to 3-inch strip of aluminum foil to prevent excessive browning; remove foil during last 15 minutes of baking. Bake until crust is golden brown, 45 to 50 minutes.

Apple Pandowdy

Pandowdies, one of the homespun American desserts with odd names, use the seasonal abundance of apples found all across this nation. The term "dowdy" refers to the practice of cutting the crust into pieces while the dessert is baking.

---

6 cups thinly sliced pared tart baking apples (about 6 medium)
½ cup sugar
½ teaspoon ground cinnamon
¼ teaspoon salt
¼ teaspoon ground nutmeg
½ cup maple-flavored syrup or light molasses
3 tablespoons water
2 tablespoons margarine or butter, melted
1 cup all-purpose flour
¼ teaspoon salt
⅓ cup shortening
3 to 4 tablespoons milk
3 tablespoons margarine or butter, melted
Cream

Heat oven to 350°. Mix apples, sugar, cinnamon, ¼ teaspoon salt and the nutmeg. Turn into ungreased 2-quart casserole. Mix syrup, water and 2 tablespoons margarine; pour over apple mixture.

Mix flour and ¼ teaspoon salt. Cut in shortening. Sprinkle in milk, 1 tablespoon at a time, mixing until all flour is moistened and pastry almost cleans side of bowl.

Gather pastry into ball; shape into flattened round on lightly floured cloth-covered board. Roll pastry to fit top of casserole with floured cloth-covered rolling pin. Place over apples in casserole; brush with 3 tablespoons melted margarine.

Bake 30 minutes; remove from oven. Cut crust into small pieces with sharp knife, mixing pieces into apple filling. Bake until apples are tender and pieces of crust are golden, about 30 minutes. Serve hot with cream. *6 servings.*

Apple Pandowdy

Deep-Dish Apple Pie

Ready in the hour or more it took New England farm families to do their morning chores, Deep-Dish Apple Pie and others like it were served for breakfast in the nineteenth century. It is a sweet and spicy treat just as it is, although there's nothing wrong with adding a slice of cheese as became customary during the 1920s.

    Pastry (below)
1½ cups sugar
  ½ cup all-purpose flour
  1 teaspoon ground nutmeg
  1 teaspoon ground cinnamon
  ¼ teaspoon salt
12 cups thinly sliced pared tart baking apples
    (about 11 medium)
  2 tablespoons margarine or butter

Heat oven to 425°. Prepare pastry. Mix sugar, flour, nutmeg, cinnamon and salt in 3-quart bowl. Stir in apples. Turn into ungreased square pan, 9×9×2 inches. Dot with margarine. Cover with crust; fold edges under just inside edges of pan. Bake until juice begins to bubble through slits in crust, about 1 hour. Serve slightly warm. *12 servings.*

Pastry

  1 cup all-purpose flour
  ½ teaspoon salt
  ⅓ cup plus 1 tablespoon shortening or ⅓ cup lard
  2 to 3 tablespoons cold water

Mix flour and salt. Cut in shortening until particles are size of small peas. Sprinkle in water, 1 tablespoon at a time, tossing with fork until all flour is moistened and pastry almost cleans side of bowl (1 to 2 teaspoons water can be added if necessary). Gather pastry into ball; shape into flattened round on lightly floured cloth-covered board. Roll into 10-inch square with floured cloth-covered rolling pin. Fold pastry into halves; cut slits near center so steam can escape.

Blueberry Slump

They say this name came about because the topping "slumps" as it's spooned into bowls for serving. The Pilgrims who settled around Plymouth found blueberries, as well as cranberries, grapes and beach plums, ready for picking. Originally, these sweetened fruit desserts with their dumpling-like toppings were cooked in a kettle suspended in the fireplace. This old-time New England dessert is always served with plenty of cream.

  ½ cup sugar
  2 tablespoons cornstarch
  ½ cup water
  1 teaspoon lemon juice
  4 cups blueberries
  1 cup all-purpose flour
  2 tablespoons sugar
1½ teaspoons baking powder
  ¼ teaspoon salt
  ¼ teaspoon ground nutmeg
  ¼ cup margarine or butter
  ⅓ cup milk
    Cream

Mix ½ cup sugar and the cornstarch in 3-quart saucepan. Stir in water and lemon juice until well blended. Stir in blueberries. Cook over medium heat, stirring constantly, until mixture thickens and boils. Boil and stir 1 minute.

Mix flour, 2 tablespoons sugar, the baking powder, salt and nutmeg. Cut in margarine until mixture resembles fine crumbs. Stir in milk. Drop dough by 6 spoonfuls onto hot blueberry mixture. Cook uncovered over low heat 10 minutes; cover and cook 10 minutes longer. Serve hot with cream. *6 servings.*

Pineapple Upside-down Cake

An invention by Henry Ginaca in 1911 that produced the ring-shaped slices of pineapple made America ready for Pineapple Upside-down Cake. By the 1920s, the cake was firmly established as one of America's favorites. Contributions to local recipe collections and entries in cooking contests included pineapple upside-down cakes in great numbers.

1/4 cup margarine or butter
1 can (20 ounces) sliced pineapple in syrup, drained (reserve 2 tablespoons syrup)
2/3 cup packed brown sugar
   Maraschino cherries, if desired
1 1/4 cups all-purpose flour or 1 1/2 cups cake flour
1 cup granulated sugar
1/3 cup shortening
3/4 cup milk
1 1/2 teaspoons baking powder
1 teaspoon vanilla
1/2 teaspoon salt
1 egg
   Sweetened whipped cream

Heat oven to 350°. Heat margarine in 9-inch ovenproof skillet or square pan, 9×9×2 inches, in oven until melted. Stir reserved pineapple syrup into margarine; sprinkle evenly with brown sugar. Arrange pineapple slices in margarine mixture. Place cherry in center of each pineapple slice.

Beat remaining ingredients except whipped cream in 3-quart bowl on low speed, scraping bowl constantly, 30 seconds. Beat on high speed, scraping bowl occasionally, 3 minutes. Pour evenly over pineapple slices.

Bake until wooden pick inserted in center comes out clean, 40 to 45 minutes. Invert on heatproof platter. Leave skillet over cake a few minutes. Serve warm with whipped cream. *9 servings.*

Apricot Upside-down Cake: Substitute 1 can (17 ounces) apricot halves for the pineapple slices.

Peach Upside-down Cake: Substitute 1 can (16 ounces) sliced peaches for the pineapple slices.

Plum Upside-down Cake: Substitute 1 can (17 ounces) plums, cut into halves and pitted, for the pineapple slices.

Bananas Foster

Another of the showy dessert recipes of New Orleans, Bananas Foster often complete an ample late morning breakfast at Brennan's restaurant in the French Quarter.

2/3 cup packed brown sugar
1/2 cup margarine or butter
1 teaspoon ground cinnamon
4 firm bananas
1/3 cup rum, brandy or orange-flavored liqueur
1 quart vanilla ice cream

Heat brown sugar, margarine and cinnamon in chafing dish or attractive skillet until sugar and margarine are melted. Cook over medium-high heat, stirring occasionally, until golden brown, about 3 minutes. Cut bananas diagonally into 1/2-inch slices; add to syrup and heat through, carefully turning slices to coat.

Heat rum in small long-handled pan just until warm; ignite and pour flaming over bananas. Stir; spoon over each serving of ice cream. *6 to 8 servings.*

Rhubarb Crisp

Where springtime comes late in northern regions of the country, rhubarb is the earliest "fruit" from the garden and a harbinger of warmer weather to come.

1⅓ cups sugar
⅓ cup all-purpose flour
½ teaspoon grated orange peel
4 cups ½-inch pieces fresh rhubarb or 1 package (16 ounces) frozen rhubarb, thawed and well drained (about 2 cups)
½ cup all-purpose flour
¼ cup packed brown sugar
¼ cup margarine or butter, softened

Heat oven to 400°. Mix sugar, ⅓ cup flour and the orange peel in 2-quart bowl; toss with rhubarb until well coated. Spread rhubarb mixture in greased square pan, 8×8×2 inches. Sprinkle any remaining sugar mixture evenly over top.

Mix ½ cup flour, the brown sugar and margarine with fork until crumbly. Sprinkle evenly over rhubarb mixture. Bake until topping is golden brown and rhubarb is tender, 35 to 40 minutes. Serve warm with ice cream or whipped cream if desired. *9 servings.*

Strawberry Shortcakes

In June, when strawberries ripen all across New England and the Midwest, any occasion can be made festive with old-fashioned Strawberry Shortcakes. Early settlers made time for events like strawberry socials, a midwestern tradition that continues today. Hot biscuits, split and buttered, are topped with sweetened strawberries and mounds of whipped cream. There are not many desserts that compare with this homegrown classic.

1 quart strawberries, sliced
1 cup sugar
2 cups all-purpose flour
2 tablespoons sugar
3 teaspoons baking powder
1 teaspoon salt
⅓ cup shortening
¾ cup milk
Margarine or butter, softened
Sweetened whipped cream

Mix strawberries and 1 cup sugar; let stand 1 hour.

Heat oven to 450°. Mix flour, 2 tablespoons sugar, the baking powder and salt. Cut in shortening until mixture resembles fine crumbs. Stir in milk just until blended. Gently smooth dough into ball on lightly floured cloth-covered board. Knead 20 to 25 times. Roll ½ inch thick; cut with floured 3-inch cutter. Place about 1 inch apart on ungreased cookie sheet. Bake until golden brown, 10 to 12 minutes.

Split shortcakes into halves while hot. Spread with margarine; fill and top with whipped cream and strawberries. *6 servings.*

Pat-in-the-Pan Shortcake: After stirring in milk, pat dough in greased round pan, 8 × 1½ inches. Bake 15 to 20 minutes.

Crème Brûlée

"Burnt cream" is the English translation for this creamy custard with carmelized sugar topping. In recent years, Californians have spooned this custard over their abundance of fruit and berries, giving new meaning to this classic dessert.

---

4 egg yolks
3 tablespoons granulated sugar
2 cups whipping cream
⅓ cup packed brown sugar
4 cups cut-up fresh fruit

Beat egg yolks in 1½-quart bowl on high speed until thick and lemon colored, about 5 minutes. Gradually beat in granulated sugar. Heat whipping cream in 2-quart saucepan over medium heat just until hot. Stir at least half of the hot cream gradually into egg yolk mixture. Stir into hot cream in saucepan. Cook over low heat, stirring constantly, until mixture thickens, 5 to 8 minutes (do not boil). Pour custard into ungreased pie plate, 9 × 1¼ inches. Cover and refrigerate at least 2 hours but no longer than 24 hours.

Set oven control to broil. Sprinkle brown sugar over custard. Broil with top about 5 inches from heat until sugar is melted and forms a glaze, about 3 minutes. Spoon over fruit. Immediately refrigerate any remaining custard. *8 servings.*

Creamy Rice Pudding

*Rice puddings are among our most nostalgic desserts. The ingredients were easily available to women in frontier settlements, where inventiveness and frugality went hand in hand. One cousin of rice pudding with the unlikely name of **Spotted Pup** — sweetened rice "spotted" with a handful of raisins — was a welcome treat of the pioneers who crossed the Great Plains by wagon train.*

⅔ cup uncooked regular rice
1⅓ cups water
2 eggs or 4 egg yolks
½ cup sugar
½ cup raisins
2 cups milk
½ teaspoon vanilla or 1 tablespoon grated orange peel
¼ teaspoon salt
Ground nutmeg

Heat rice and water to boiling, stirring once or twice; reduce heat. Cover and simmer 14 minutes. (Do not lift cover or stir.) All water should be absorbed.

Heat oven to 325°. Beat eggs in ungreased 1½-quart casserole. Stir in sugar, raisins, milk, vanilla, salt and hot rice; sprinkle with nutmeg. Bake uncovered, stirring occasionally, until knife inserted halfway between center and edge comes out clean, 50 to 60 minutes. Serve warm or cold and, if desired, with cream. Immediately refrigerate any remaining pudding. *6 to 8 servings.*

Spiced Flan

Flans, the traditional caramel-topped custards of Mexico, are the perfect soothing end to a meal featuring spicy foods from the American Southwest. This recipe has a subtle spiciness of its own due to additions of nutmeg, cinnamon, allspice and a touch of brandy.

¾ cup sugar
2 tablespoons water
½ cup sugar
2 eggs, slightly beaten
2 tablespoons brandy, if desired
½ teaspoon vanilla
¼ teaspoon ground nutmeg
¼ teaspoon ground cinnamon
¼ teaspoon ground allspice
   Dash of salt
2 cups milk (scalded then cooled)

Heat oven to 350°. Heat ¾ cup sugar in heavy 1-quart saucepan over low heat, stirring constantly, until sugar is melted and golden brown. Gradually stir in water. Divide syrup evenly among six 6-ounce custard cups. Allow syrup to harden in cups about 10 minutes.

Mix ½ cup sugar, the eggs, brandy, vanilla, nutmeg, cinnamon, allspice and salt. Gradually stir in milk. Pour custard mixture over syrup. Place cups in rectangular pan, 13 × 9 × 2 inches, on oven rack. Pour very hot water into pan to within ½ inch of tops of cups. Bake until knife inserted halfway between center and edge comes out clean, about 45 minutes.

Remove cups from water. Refrigerate at least 4 hours but no longer than 24 hours. To unmold, carefully loosen side of custard with knife or small spatula. Place dessert dish or plate on top of cup and, holding tightly, invert dish and cup. Shake cup gently to loosen and remove. Immediately refrigerate any remaining custard. *6 servings.*

Bread Pudding with Whiskey Sauce

America's home cooking revival has rekindled interest in this favorite from grandma's kitchen. Bread pudding is most associated with Louisiana cooking when served with Whiskey Sauce.

---

2 cups milk
¼ cup margarine or butter
½ cup sugar
1 teaspoon ground cinnamon or nutmeg
¼ teaspoon salt
2 eggs, slightly beaten
6 cups dry bread cubes (8 slices bread)
½ cup raisins, if desired
   Whiskey Sauce (below)

Heat oven to 350°. Heat milk and margarine over medium heat until margarine is melted and milk is scalded. Mix sugar, cinnamon, salt and eggs in 3-quart bowl; stir in bread cubes and raisins. Stir in milk mixture; pour into ungreased 1½-quart casserole. Place casserole in pan of very hot water (1 inch deep). Bake until knife inserted 1 inch from edge of casserole comes out clean, 40 to 45 minutes. Prepare Whiskey Sauce; serve with warm bread pudding. *8 servings.*

Whiskey Sauce

Heat 1 cup packed brown sugar, ½ cup margarine or butter and 3 to 4 tablespoons bourbon to boiling in 1-quart heavy saucepan over medium heat, stirring constantly.

Bread Pudding with Whiskey Sauce

Strawberry Ice Cream, Chocolate Ice Cream

Strawberry Ice Cream

Philadelphia is most associated with America's first taste of ice cream. George Washington bought a "Cream Machine for Making Ice" in 1784 and was among those in the nation's first capital who popularized what has become our favorite dessert.

3 egg yolks, beaten
½ cup sugar
1 cup milk
¼ teaspoon salt
2 cups chilled whipping cream
1 teaspoon vanilla
1 pint strawberries
½ cup sugar
   Few drops red food color, if desired

Mix egg yolks, ½ cup sugar, the milk and salt. Cook over medium heat, stirring constantly, just until bubbles appear around edge. Refrigerate in chilled bowl until room temperature, 2 to 3 hours.

Stir whipping cream and vanilla into milk mixture. Mash strawberries and ½ cup sugar; stir into milk mixture. Mix in food color. Pour into freezer can; put dasher in place. Cover and adjust crank. Place can in freezer tub. Fill freezer tub ⅓ full of ice; add remaining ice alternately with layers of rock salt (6 parts ice to 1 part rock salt). Turn crank until it turns with difficulty. Drain water from freezer tub. Remove lid; take out dasher. Pack mixture down; replace lid. Repack in ice and rock salt. Let stand several hours to ripen. *1 quart ice cream.*

Peach Ice Cream, Vanilla Bean Ice Cream, Nut Brittle Ice Cream

Chocolate Ice Cream: Omit strawberries, ½ cup sugar and the food color. Increase sugar in cooked mixture to 1 cup. Beat 2 squares (1 ounce each) unsweetened chocolate, melted, into milk mixture before cooking.

Nut Brittle Ice Cream: Omit strawberries, ½ cup sugar and the food color. Increase vanilla to 1 tablespoon. Stir 1 cup crushed almond, pecan or peanut brittle into milk mixture after adding vanilla.

Peach Ice Cream: Omit strawberries and food color. Mash 4 or 5 peaches to yield 2 cups. Stir ½ cup sugar into peaches; stir into milk mixture after adding vanilla.

Vanilla Bean Ice Cream: Omit vanilla, strawberries, ½ cup sugar and the food color. Add 3-inch piece of vanilla bean to milk mixture before cooking. Before cooling, remove bean and split lengthwise into halves. Scrape seeds into cooked mixture with tip of small knife; discard bean.

Vanilla Ice Cream: Omit strawberries, ½ cup sugar and the food color. Increase vanilla to 1 tablespoon.

Lindy's Cheesecake

*The famous cheesecakes we associate with urban settings like New York City have their roots in the country cheese pies and **kuchens** of immigrants from England and Central Europe.*

---

        1 cup all-purpose flour
      1/2 cup margarine or butter, softened
      1/4 cup sugar
        1 tablespoon grated lemon peel
        1 egg yolk
        5 packages (8 ounces each) cream cheese, softened
    1¾ cups sugar
        3 tablespoons all-purpose flour
        1 tablespoon grated orange peel
        1 tablespoon grated lemon peel
      1/4 teaspoon salt
        5 eggs
        2 egg yolks
      1/4 cup whipping cream
      3/4 cup whipping cream

Heat oven to 400°. Lightly grease springform pan, 9 × 3 inches; remove bottom. Mix 1 cup flour, the margarine, 1/4 cup sugar, 1 tablespoon lemon peel and 1 egg yolk with hands. Press 1/3 of the mixture evenly on bottom of pan; place on cookie sheet. Bake until golden, 8 to 10 minutes; cool. Assemble bottom and side of pan; secure side. Press remaining mixture all the way up side of pan.

Heat oven to 475°. Beat cream cheese, 1¾ cups sugar, 3 tablespoons flour, the orange peel, 1 tablespoon lemon peel, the salt and two of the eggs in 3-quart bowl until smooth. Continue beating, adding remaining eggs and 2 egg yolks, one at a time. Beat in 1/4 cup whipping cream on low speed. Pour into pan. Bake 15 minutes. Reduce oven temperature to 200°. Bake 1 hour. Turn off oven; leave cheesecake in oven 15 minutes. Cover and refrigerate at least 12 hours but no longer than 48 hours.

Loosen cheesecake from side of pan; remove side of pan. Beat 3/4 cup whipping cream in chilled bowl until stiff. Spread whipped cream over top of cheesecake. Immediately refrigerate any remaining cheesecake. *20 servings.*

Deluxe Brownies

Brownies became popular in the 1920s. Some say brownies were originally a fallen chocolate cake. Others believe brownies are an American version of Scottish cocoa scones. Whatever the origin, the first brownies in the United States were called Bangor Brownies after the city in Maine where they were discovered.

      2/3 cup margarine or butter
        5 squares (1 ounce each) unsweetened chocolate, cut into pieces
    1¾ cups sugar
        2 teaspoons vanilla
        3 eggs
        1 cup all-purpose flour
        1 cup chopped nuts

Heat oven to 350°. Heat margarine and chocolate over low heat, stirring constantly, until melted; cool slightly. Beat sugar, vanilla and eggs on high speed 5 minutes. Beat in chocolate mixture on low speed. Beat in flour just until blended. Stir in nuts. Spread in greased square pan, 9 × 9 × 2 inches. Bake just until brownies begin to pull away from sides of pan, 40 to 45 minutes; cool. Cut into 2-inch squares. *16 brownies.*

Farm-style Oatmeal Cookies

Oatmeal cookies have long filled country cookie jars with the kind of nourishing snack farm women liked to provide their families. These classic American cookies and a mug of hot chocolate make the perfect treat after outdoor chores on a blustery day.

---

2 cups packed brown sugar
1 cup lard or shortening
½ cup buttermilk
1 teaspoon vanilla
4 cups quick-cooking oats
1¾ cups all-purpose or whole wheat flour
1 teaspoon baking soda
¾ teaspoon salt

Heat oven to 375°. Mix brown sugar, lard, buttermilk and vanilla in 3-quart bowl. Stir in remaining ingredients. Shape dough into 1-inch balls. Place about 3 inches apart on ungreased cookie sheet. Flatten cookies with bottom of glass dipped in water. Bake until golden brown, 8 to 10 minutes. Immediately remove from cookie sheet. *About 7 dozen cookies.*

Mexican Wedding Cakes

These melt-in-your-mouth cookies go by many names in the recipe collections of American cooks. They are special enough for celebrations of all kinds!

---

1 cup margarine or butter, softened
½ cup powdered sugar
1 teaspoon vanilla
2¼ cups all-purpose flour
¾ cup finely chopped nuts
¼ teaspoon salt
Powdered sugar

Heat oven to 400°. Mix margarine, ½ cup powdered sugar and the vanilla in 3-quart bowl. Stir in flour, nuts and salt. Shape dough into 1-inch balls. Bake on ungreased cookie sheet until set but not brown, 8 to 9 minutes. Roll in powdered sugar while warm. Cool; roll in powdered sugar again. *About 4 dozen cookies.*

Chocolate Chip Cookies

Chocolate chip cookies date back to the 1930s when Ruth Wakefield of the Toll House Inn in Whitman, Massachusetts, chopped a bar of leftover semisweet chocolate and added the pieces to dough for Butter Drop Cookies, a basic cookie recipe from Colonial America. The cookies with the little chunks of chocolate throughout them made the news all over New England. Within a short time the cookies were popular coast to coast and one of the nation's leading chocolate companies was marketing the specially shaped chocolate pieces used for the cookies today.

---

1 cup margarine or butter, softened
¾ cup granulated sugar
¾ cup packed brown sugar
1 egg
2¼ cups all-purpose flour
1 teaspoon baking soda
½ teaspoon salt
1 cup coarsely chopped nuts
1 package (12 ounces) semisweet chocolate chips

Heat oven to 375°. Mix margarine, sugars and egg. Stir in flour, baking soda and salt (dough will be stiff). Stir in nuts and chocolate chips. Drop dough by rounded teaspoonfuls about 2 inches apart onto ungreased cookie sheet. Bake until light brown, 8 to 10 minutes. (Centers will be soft.) Cool slightly; remove from cookie sheet. *About 6 dozen cookies.*

Snickerdoodles

Just one of a long line of American cookies with whimsical names, these cookies first appear in the recipe collections of the Dutch who settled New York's Hudson River region where they were known as **Schnecken Noodles**. *These crinkle-topped cookies rolled in cinnamon and sugar are both fun to say and fun to eat!*

1½ cups sugar
 ½ cup margarine or butter, softened
 ½ cup shortening
 2 eggs
2¾ cups all-purpose flour
 2 teaspoons cream of tartar
 1 teaspoon baking soda
 ¼ teaspoon salt
 2 tablespoons sugar
 2 teaspoons ground cinnamon

Heat oven to 400°. Mix 1½ cups sugar, the margarine, shortening and eggs thoroughly in 3-quart bowl. Stir in flour, cream of tartar, baking soda and salt until blended. Shape dough by rounded teaspoonfuls into balls.

Mix 2 tablespoons sugar and the cinnamon; roll balls in sugar mixture. Place about 2 inches apart on ungreased cookie sheet. Bake until set, 8 to 10 minutes. Immediately remove from cookie sheet. *About 6 dozen cookies.*

Joe Froggers

Virtually every generation of American children has enjoyed cookies flavored with ginger and molasses. German and Dutch settlers in New York and Pennsylvania baked large ginger cookies shaped like people, and crisp gingersnaps, but a man named Uncle Joe who lived in a cabin by a pond in Marblehead, Massachusetts, gets credit for these fanciful, sugar-dusted rounds. Local fishermen who bought Uncle Joe's large flat ginger cookies gave them the name Joe Froggers because they reminded them of the equally large, fat frogs that resided in his pond.

---

 1 cup sugar
 ½ cup shortening
 1 cup dark molasses
 ½ cup water
 4 cups all-purpose flour
1½ teaspoons salt
1½ teaspoons ground ginger
 1 teaspoon baking soda
 ½ teaspoon ground cloves
 ½ teaspoon ground nutmeg
 ¼ teaspoon ground allspice
    Sugar

Mix 1 cup sugar, the shortening, molasses and water in 3-quart bowl. Stir in remaining ingredients except sugar. Cover and refrigerate at least 2 hours.

Heat oven to 375°. Roll dough ¼ inch thick on well-floured cloth-covered board. Cut into 3-inch circles; sprinkle with sugar. Place about 1½ inches apart on ungreased cookie sheet. Bake until almost no indentation remains when touched, 10 to 12 minutes. Cool 2 minutes; remove from cookie sheet. Cool completely. *About 3 dozen cookies.*

Soldier's Fudge

*When Eliza Doolittle makes her plea for "lots of chocolate for me to eat" in **My Fair Lady**, her sentiment is one that's been shared by generations of homesick servicemen and servicewomen. Soldier's Fudge is one of those word-of-mouth recipes that swept the country during World War II. Besides being a good shipper and luscious to eat, the fudge contained no sugar — a bonus in World War II because of sugar rationing.*

---

1 can (14 ounces) sweetened condensed milk
1 package (12 ounces) semisweet chocolate chips
1 square (1 ounce) unsweetened chocolate, coarsely chopped, if desired
1½ cups chopped nuts, if desired
1 teaspoon vanilla

Butter square pan, 8 × 8 × 2 inches. Heat milk, chocolate chips and unsweetened chocolate over low heat, stirring constantly, until chocolate is melted and mixture is smooth; remove from heat. Stir in nuts and vanilla. Spread in pan. Refrigerate until firm. Cut into 1-inch squares. *64 candies.*

Pralines

The origin of Pralines is traced to a French diplomat named Plessis-Praslin, whose butler prepared special sugar-coated almonds to cure his master's indigestion. Whether they succeeded isn't known, but his recipe came to America with the French settlers of New Orleans. Using native pecans and brown sugar, the Creoles' adaptation of that cure became their most famous confection, perhaps the sweetest of all sweets.

---

2 cups packed light brown sugar
1 cup granulated sugar
1¼ cups milk
¼ cup light corn syrup
⅛ teaspoon salt
1 teaspoon vanilla
1½ cups pecan halves (5½ ounces)

Heat sugars, milk, corn syrup and salt to boiling in 3-quart saucepan, stirring constantly. Cook, without stirring, to 236° on candy thermometer (or until small amount of mixture dropped into very cold water forms a soft ball that flattens when removed from water). Immediately remove thermometer. Cool, without stirring, until saucepan is cool to touch, about 1½ hours.

Add vanilla and pecans. Beat with spoon until mixture is slightly thickened and just coats pecans but does not lose its gloss, about 1 minute. Drop by spoonfuls onto waxed paper. (Try to divide pecans equally.) Cool until candies are firm and no longer glossy, 12 to 18 hours. Wrap individually in plastic wrap or waxed paper and store tightly covered at room temperature. *About 1½ dozen candies.*

Penuche

*Penuche sometimes goes by the name, brown sugar fudge, because that is exactly what it is. **Panocha** or **panucha** are both terms from Spanish words that refer to a coarse brown sugar found in Mexico.*

1 cup granulated sugar
1 cup packed brown sugar
⅔ cup milk
2 tablespoons corn syrup
¼ teaspoon salt
2 tablespoons margarine or butter
1 teaspoon vanilla
½ cup coarsely chopped nuts, if desired

Butter loaf pan, 9 × 5 × 3 inches. Heat sugars, milk, corn syrup and salt to boiling in 2-quart saucepan over medium heat, stirring constantly, until sugars are dissolved. Boil, stirring occasionally, to 234° on candy thermometer (or until small amount of mixture dropped into very cold water forms a soft ball that flattens when removed from water). Remove from heat; stir in margarine. Cool mixture, without stirring, to 120° or until bottom of saucepan is lukewarm.

Add vanilla. Beat with wooden spoon until thick and no longer glossy, 5 to 10 minutes. (Mixture will hold its shape when dropped from spoon.) Quickly stir in nuts. Spread evenly in pan. Cool until firm. Cut into 1-inch squares. *32 candies.*

Peanut Brittle

The most popular peanut recipe in America is probably for peanut brittle. It is just one of the ways to serve this Southern specialty, which is not really a nut at all. The peanut plant is related to other legumes like peas and may explain one of the peanut's aliases, goober peas.

1½ teaspoons baking soda
1 teaspoon water
1 teaspoon vanilla
1½ cups sugar
1 cup water
1 cup light corn syrup
3 tablespoons margarine or butter
1 pound shelled unroasted peanuts

Butter 2 cookie sheets, 15½ × 12 inches; keep warm. Mix baking soda, 1 teaspoon water and the vanilla; reserve. Mix sugar, 1 cup water and the corn syrup in 3-quart saucepan. Cook over medium heat, stirring occasionally, to 240° on candy thermometer (or until small amount of mixture dropped into very cold water forms a soft ball that flattens when removed from water).

Stir in margarine and peanuts. Cook, stirring constantly, to 300° (or until small amount of mixture dropped into very cold water separates into threads that are hard and brittle). Watch carefully so mixture does not burn. Immediately remove from heat; stir in baking soda mixture.

Pour half of the candy mixture onto each cookie sheet and quickly spread about ¼ inch thick; cool. Break into pieces. *About 6 dozen candies.*

Index